THE GREAT NORTHERN EXPRESS

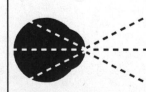

This Large Print Book carries the
Seal of Approval of N.A.V.H.

THE GREAT NORTHERN EXPRESS

A WRITER'S JOURNEY HOME

HOWARD FRANK MOSHER

THORNDIKE PRESS

A part of Gale, Cengage Learning

SAYVILLE LIBRARY

GALE
CENGAGE Learning·

Detroit • New York • San Francisco • New Haven, Conn • Waterville, Maine • London

GALE
CENGAGE Learning®

Copyright © 2012 by Howard Frank Mosher.
Grateful acknowledgment is made to The New England Press, Inc. for permission to reprint "The Trouble with a Son," "The Waves," and "Senior Year" from *Star in the Shed Window: Collected Poems 1933–1988* by James Hayford (Shelburne, VT. The New England Press, Inc. 1989)
Thorndike Press, a part of Gale, Cengage Learning.

ALL RIGHTS RESERVED
Thorndike Press® Large Print Nonfiction.
The text of this Large Print edition is unabridged.
Other aspects of the book may vary from the original edition.
Set in 16 pt. Plantin.

LIBRARY OF CONGRESS CATALOGING-IN-PUBLICATION DATA

Mosher, Howard Frank.
  The great northern express : a writer's journey home / by Howard Frank Mosher.
    pages ; cm. — (Thorndike Press large print nonfiction)
    ISBN-13: 978-1-4104-4870-5 (hardcover)
    ISBN-10: 1-4104-4870-3 (hardcover)
    1. Mosher, Howard Frank. 2. Novelists, American—21st century—Biography. 3. Large type books. I. Title.
    PS3563.O8844Z46 2012
    813'.54—dc23
    [B]   2012008807

Published in 2012 by arrangement with Crown Publishers, a division of Random House, Inc.

Printed in the United States of America
1 2 3 4 5 6 7 16 15 14 13 12

For my grandchildren,

Frank James Williamson
and
True Hilton Williamson

INTRODUCTION

The Great Northern Express is a tale not of two cities but, give or take a few, of one hundred. Specifically, it is the story of the monumental book tour I made the summer I turned sixty-five. That journey was inspired by a much shorter trip: a walk up the street to our village's tiny post office, where I received an unexpected letter.

This is also the story of how my wife, Phillis, and I came to settle in the Northeast Kingdom of Vermont. It, too, began with a journey: this one when we were just twenty-one, to interview for teaching jobs in the remote mill town of Orleans, in the northern Green Mountains just south of the Canadian border, where we planned to teach for a year or two, save some money, and then move on to graduate school.

I have divided *The Great Northern Express* into three parts: Faith, Hope, and Love. Certainly, faith, hope, and love are what sustained me during a sojourn I feared might be my last. The sixty-five chapters here suggest how, upon reaching an age when many people think about retiring, or already have, I set out to rededicate myself to what has been my profession for more than four decades. Since I am, by both trade and personal inclination, a storyteller, each chapter tells a story.

I have changed the names of a few of the people I have written about. In two or three cases I combined characters to further conceal actual identities. Like Henry David Thoreau, who in fact spent slightly more than two years at Walden Pond, which he compressed into one calendar year in *Walden,* I have also occasionally used experiences from earlier or later times in my life.

The Great Northern Express is the story of how, as I traveled from coast to coast and border to border in the summer of my sixty-fifth year, two journeys seemed to meld into the narrative of one writer's search, in his life and work, for the true meaning of home.

■ ■ ■ ■

PART I
FAITH

■ ■ ■ ■

1
THE TRIP NOT TAKEN

My first home was a ghost town. Hidden away in a remote hollow of the Catskill Mountains, the company-owned hamlet of Chichester went bankrupt in 1939, three years before I was born. A few families, ours included, hung on for several more years. But without its once-prosperous furniture factory, which reopened a couple of times in my early boyhood only to shut down a few months later, Chichester was just another dying upstate mill town. By the time I turned five, the place was on its last legs, and looked it.

While many of my happiest memories date from those years in the Catskills — I caught my first trout in the stream behind our house when I was four, shagged foul balls for older kids at the overgrown diamond on the village green — from the fall when I entered first grade until my first year of high school, my family moved, by my count, ten times. My dad, a schoolteacher, had itchy feet, like Pa Ingalls in Laura Ingalls Wilder's *Little House* books. After leaving Chichester, we Moshers would strike out for new territory every year or so. And although I never wanted to leave any of the towns where we temporarily alighted, I don't recall thinking there was anything unusual about pulling up stakes at the end of every school year and relocating. In those days I was a ball-playing, daydreaming, reading little guy with a slew of imaginary companions, mostly from the books I devoured — Huck Finn, *Treasure Island*'s Jim Hawkins, David Copperfield. So long as our family stayed together and I could find a nearby trout brook, a ball field, and a steady supply of books to read, I didn't care how often we moved.

Still, I have always regarded Chichester as my hometown. If asked for a favorite early memory, I'd recall sitting between my dad and Reg Bennett in the front seat of Dad's old, battleship-gray DeSoto on the mountaintop behind our house, trying to dial in the Yankees–Red Sox game on the car radio. As the house lights of the town below began to wink on in the twilight, and Mel Allen or Curt Gowdy waxed poetic about the Bronx Bombers or the boys from Beantown, Reg

12

and Dad would talk baseball. Reg — my father's best friend, fishing partner, and teaching colleague — was a second father and honorary uncle to me. In temperament, Dad and Reg were as different from each other as lifelong friends can be. My father was a big, outgoing, nonjudgmental man, comfortable with himself and others. A natural leader, he caught for the Chichester town baseball team, as he had for his high school nine. Reg was slighter in build and was several inches shorter. He was combative and, if wronged, quick to pick a fight. He pitched for the Chichester team. Over the years he had perfected a hard-breaking curve, which he could and frequently did use to brush aggressive hitters back from the plate or knock them down. Like my grandfather Mosher, my father had a romantic outlook on life, which I have inherited. Reg, for his part, was a realist, with an ironical turn of mind and a dry sense of humor that I loved.

Reg loved to argue. My father did not. Sooner or later, though, Dad would be drawn into a debate, amicable enough at first, often over the relative merits of their two favorite players. Dad, a true-blue Yankee fan, was a Joe DiMaggio man. Reg was a devotee of Ted Williams. As the evening wore on and the game became heated — as Yankee–Red Sox games are wont to do — the baseball arguments between my father and uncle intensified. Soon they'd both get mad, stop addressing each other directly, and begin arguing by proxy, through me.

"Howard Frank," my uncle said — as a boy, I was often addressed by both names to distinguish me from my father, Howard Hudson — "Howard Frank, I am here to tell you that Ted Williams is the greatest pure hitter in the history of the game."

"Maybe so, Howard Frank," my father shot back. "But you have my permission to inform your uncle that Joe DiMaggio is the most complete *all-around* player in the history of the game."

I usually said nothing. For one thing, I was only four. Also, though I already had a keen appreciation for my relatives' many eccentricities, I didn't like arguments any more than Dad did. Fortunately, about the time full darkness settled in, we would lose the radio broadcast altogether. Then I would ask my uncle to tell me a story.

"Tell me a story" was my mantra, and Reg knew scores of good ones. Stories of the old bear hunters, ginseng gatherers, mountain guides, hermits, witches, and pioneer families who had settled Chichester. Like the Northeast Kingdom of Vermont when Phillis and I first arrived in the mid-1960s, Chichester in the '40s and '50s was a gold mine of stories. My feisty uncle was its Homer, as well as my first storytelling mentor. Reg was working on an anecdotal history of Chichester, and sometimes he would read aloud to me from the manuscript.

Of all Reg's stories, my favorite was the one that hadn't yet happened. That was his description of the road trip he and I would take the summer I turned twenty-one. We'd start out in Robert Frost's New England, then head for New York City, where my uncle's favorite *New Yorker* writer, Joseph Mitchell, had chronicled the lives of his beloved gypsies, street preachers, and fish vendors. We'd visit the New York Public Library on Fifth Avenue and Forty-first Street, with its two stone lions guarding the main entrance. Next we'd strike out for the Great Smokies, Thomas Wolfe country — my uncle loved *You Can't Go Home Again* and *Look Homeward, Angel.* We'd drop by Oxford, Mississippi, and have a gander at Faulkner's home, slope down to Marjorie Kinnan Rawlings's (*The Yearling*) Florida. Then we'd head for the American West — Reg, a huge fan of Zane Grey, would read

15

me Grey's Westerns by the hour. We'd walk the streets of Raymond Chandler's LA and Dashiell Hammett's San Francisco, check out James T. Farrell's Chicago (with a side visit to the Windy City's great bookstore, Brentano's,) take a look at Hemingway's upper Michigan and Aldo Leopold's Wisconsin. We'd eat at greasy spoons and roadside custard stands, stay at motor courts and tourist cabins. Throw our fly rods and baseball gloves in the backseat and see a ball game in every town that had a team.

Our long-planned trip was no pipe dream, but my uncle and I never got to take that literary odyssey. By the time I turned twenty-one and graduated from college, Reg's wife, my aunt Elsie, wasn't well, and I'd gotten married and taken a teaching job in northern Vermont. Writing my way from book to book and decade to decade, I set most of my own fiction in my adopted Northeast Kingdom. I turned fifty. Then sixty. Approaching my sixty-fifth birthday, with regrets for the trip not taken, I began to feel that I had to do it now or never.

Then, in the late autumn of my sixty-fifth year, came the walk to the post office that would change my life forever.

16

2
MY MACARTHUR
FELLOWSHIP ARRIVES

MacArthur Fellowships are designed for talented individuals who have shown exceptional originality and dedication in their creative pursuits.
— GUIDELINES OF THE JOHN D. AND CATHERINE T. MACARTHUR FELLOWSHIP

In this era of instant text messaging and walk-around cell phones clamped to our ears like alien appendages, most news, good and otherwise, arrives quickly. Still, I am certain that when my MacArthur Fellowship arrives, it will do so the old-fashioned way, by U.S. mail. One morning I will set out on my regular six-days-a-week walk to the post office, and there the notification will be. Likely it will come in a cream-colored envelope constructed of the highest-grade linen. My full name will appear on the front, perhaps with an "Esquire" tacked on in deference to a soon-to-be-Fellow. The

17

foundation's return address will be stamped in a discreet but stately font across the sealed flap on the back.

Some years ago I heard that the Mac-Arthur Fellowship carried a stipend of $350,000. Recently, someone told me they'd gone up to half a mil.

"That ought to cover the gas for our cross-country trip," I said on my way to the post office to pick up my grant that fateful fall morning.

You see, I still like to talk out loud to myself. And to the gallery of companions that my mother tells me I've had since I was two. I will rattle along for hours on end to relatives living and deceased, friends and adversaries, other writers, even some favorite fictional characters, like rangers Gus McCrae and Woodrow Call from *Lonesome Dove.* This morning I was conversing with my storytelling mentor, Uncle Reg, who had passed away fifteen years before.

Suddenly, an onrushing eighteen-wheeler blasted its air horn. Preoccupied by my conversation with Reg, I'd come within half a step of launching myself into the path of a log truck.

"That was close," the postmaster said to me.

"I don't know what I was thinking."

"You seemed to be talking to someone."

"Yes. I was . . . practicing. For an upcoming interview."

As I had expected — expected for the last twenty-five years, or so — here was the long-awaited cream-colored envelope. Why prolong the suspense? I tore the thing open with trembling fingers. But wait. So far from a "Dear Mr. Mosher, The John D. and Catherine T. MacArthur Foundation is delighted to inform you that you have been awarded . . . ," so far from a notification that if I so chose, I could spend the rest of my life crisscrossing the United States in commemoration of the trip my uncle and I never made, what I found myself scanning was a notice from my physician informing me that the prostate count from my annual bloodwork was high. Anything over 4.0 can indicate cancerous activity. "See me immediately," she had scrawled beside the 5.9 reading.

"There it is, at long last," said my uncle.

"There is *what?*" I said.

"Your MacArthur Fellowship," he said. Then, "You need to have that taken care of right away, Howard Frank. Prostate cancer kills thirty thousand men a year in this country."

3
TREATMENT

Both of my paternal grandparents died of cancer, as did my dad's younger sister. My mother — now ninety-six and living on her own, just up the street from our house — has survived both breast and bladder cancer. But right here and now, I want to tell you that this is not a medical memoir. Nor is it, believe you me, an inspirational memoir extolling how, with the help of a brilliant doctor, a breakthrough procedure in radiation therapy, and a supportive family, I licked prostate cancer. Though in fact, with the help of a brilliant doctor, a remarkable new development in medical technology, and a very loving family, I *may* have done just that.

In the grand old Mosher family tradition of high-spirited hopefulness, combined with what a book critic once called a "lunatic sense of humor," I immediately began referring to my disorder, and to the treatment that followed, as my personal MacArthur Fellowship. The euphemism struck me as delightfully ghoulish, along the lines of the ancient Greeks referring to their gods' dreaded and relentless agents of revenge as the "gentle" Furies.

For the record, I will report that I had two gold bands about the size of ordinary staples fired into my ailing organ. The prostate gland is something of a gadabout. This free spirit of the male pelvic region floats around with an altogether cavalier insouciance, sometimes rubbing molecules with other organs that you decidedly do not want bombarded by millions of killer X-rays. The thin gold bands enable the radiation machine to determine the precise location of the peripatetic prostate before each treatment.

Next came forty-four ten-minute sessions at the Norris Cotton Cancer Clinic in Hanover and St. Johnsbury, supervised by Dr. John Marshall, a renowned radiation oncologist who interned under a former student of Marie Curie. Also an award-winning team of nurses and technicians who were as supportive of this talking-out-loud-to-himself storyteller as they were ruthless in their scorched-earth assault on those voracious little night-of-the-living-dead cells that can, if they start to spread, kill a man in a few short months.

Other than some "increased frequency," by which I mean that, when driving, I had to stop to pee about every eight miles, I coasted through the first trimester of my fellowship period without much apparent difficulty. It occurred to me that my attempt at dark humor actually made good sense. A brush with any potentially fatal illness can be a wake-up call, a reminder — as if we needed one — of our mortality, and an opportunity. In a way, my personal MacArthur was better than a real one. What good would half a million bucks from the magnanimous John D. and Catherine T. outfit do me if I had only three months to spend it before bidding my family and friends a tearful farewell?

In fact, my treatment gave me something infinitely more precious than cash — it gave me time, though the jury was still out on how much. Now, what would I do with it?

4
I DECIDE TO HIT THE ROAD

From the MacArthur Foundation guide-lines:

1. RECIPIENTS MAY ADVANCE THEIR EX-PERTISE.

For a novelist, expertise is a tricky proposi-tion. Each time I start a new novel, I have to teach myself how to write one all over again. Like confidence, and the women speaking of Michelangelo in the T. S. Eliot poem, expertise comes and goes, with mad-dening unpredictability. In the fiction-writing game, there is no equivalent to the little gold staples implanted deep in my gut.

2. ENGAGE IN BOLD NEW WORK.

I was willing to keep this possibility in mind. But I'd already started work on a new Civil War novel with a young firebrand from Vermont as its hero. How much bold new work could one writer handle at once?

3. CHANGE FIELDS.

Nope. At sixty-four I didn't have the faintest notion how to *do* anything else. I hadn't held down a job in the real world for more than thirty years. What's more, writing isn't merely my "field." It defines who I am. Too late to change fields now.

4. ALTER THE DIRECTION OF THEIR CAREER.

At last we were getting somewhere. Writing may well be a glorious profession, but it's a hellishly uncertain career. Anything I could do to alter my decades-long holding pattern would have to be an improvement.

That spring, as I reclined under my new friend, the gigantic, humming Varian Clinac 2100 EX radiation machine that was frying my prostate gland and God knows what else to a crisp, I began thinking that maybe the time had come to *alter the direction of my career.*

I love to travel cross-country. Seeing new territory delights me, as does visiting bookstores. The June publication date for my latest novel would be within a week of my final radiation treatment and my sixty-fifth birthday, and as the date approached, I became increasingly excited. Why not combine my

24

long-delayed uncle-nephew road trip with a book tour? And not just any book tour. Instead of the usual perfunctory, eight-city flying tour, I would drive, both to see the country, as my uncle and I had planned, and to stop at bookstores in smaller cities as well as the bigger ones. I'd economize by touring in my twenty-year-old Chevy Celebrity, with 280,000 miles on the odometer, the vehicle I often referred to as the Loser Cruiser. I would, by God, spend the entire summer out on the open road promoting my new novel, on what I was already thinking of as the Great American Book Tour. An adventure that might, with luck, enable me not only to alter the direction of my writing career but to gain a fresh perspective on what I loved enough to live for in the time I had left.

5
HAROLD WHO CALLS AHEAD

"Hi, there. This is the novelist Howard Frank Mosher."

Silence.

I soldiered on. "May I please speak with your bookstore events coordinator?"

"Yeah, well. That would be me. I guess."

"Terrific. I'll be publishing my tenth book this summer, and I'm putting together, if you can believe such a thing, a one-hundred-city book tour. Let's see, I'll be in New Mexico in the second week of July. I was hoping we could arrange —"

"Who'd you say this was?"

"Howard Mosher? The novelist?" Good grief. Could I possibly be losing momentum already?

"Harold who?"

"*Howard.* Howard Frank Mosher."

"So are you a local author or what?"

"Well, actually, I'm from Vermont, but —"

"*Vermont?*" The events coordinator, who

26

might have been all of fifteen, could hardly have sounded more outraged if I'd announced I was from Guantánamo.

"Hey, Harold. I'm with a customer. Okay? E-mail me."

"Howard."

"Say what?"

"It's *Howard.* Not Harold."

Mercifully for us both, the line went dead.

Scores of phone calls later, by virtue of sheer, bullheaded stubbornness, I had somehow managed to set up about one hundred and fifty book events in one hundred or so towns and cities nationwide. In introducing my new novel to the overflowing audiences that I would no doubt attract, I had decided to start by talking about my life and work in the place I have long called Kingdom County. I might even show some slides. That was it! For my old-fashioned Great American Book Tour, I would put together an old-fashioned slide show. I'd call it "Where in the World Is Kingdom County?"

"Go for it," Phillis said. "There are worse things to promote than novels."

"Like what?"

She thought for a moment. "Amway products?"

"It's come to this, then," Reg said to me a week later as we headed up the sidewalk toward my friend Linda Ramsdell's renowned Galaxy Bookshop in Hardwick, Vermont, for the launch party of my new book.

"Lighten up," I replied, to the consternation of the polite elderly gentleman who had offered to carry my slide projector into the store.

The milestone that authors work for years to read was at hand. Publication date. And, for me and my ever-present uncle, the eve of an adventure we'd been waiting half a century for.

6
WHERE IN THE WORLD IS KINGDOM COUNTY?

It was the last day of April 1964, and Phillis and I were headed from the rolling farm country of central New York to the mountains of northeastern Vermont to interview for teaching jobs. In less than a month, Phillis would receive her degree from Syracuse University in science education. She would then be qualified to teach biology and earth science. With luck I might be awarded a degree from the liberal arts college. Though I'd majored in English and had always, from the time I was six or seven, planned to become a writer, a teller of tales like those my parents read to me by Mark Twain and Charles Dickens, I was not qualified to do much of anything. Still, we planned to be married that August. We needed to earn some money, and after that, our future was open-ended. Perhaps we'd go on to graduate school. Scarcely more than a kid myself, I was naive enough to suppose that somewhere, maybe at one of the MFA creative writing programs that were becoming popular at American universities, I would find a blueprint for how to write stories that someone besides my mother might want to read.

We'd learned about two teaching vacancies in a tiny town in Vermont. Though we had no idea what or exactly where the Northeast Kingdom was, we'd found Orleans on a Vermont road map, been intrigued by the sparsely populated terrain, the mountains, the numerous lakes and streams, and decided to drive up and have a look. If nothing else, it would be a fine spring lark.

In Burlington the maple trees were beginning to leaf out. Daffodils were blooming on the quadrangle of the university. Students in shorts lounged on the newly green grass. But as we continued northeast over the Green Mountains, the maple buds were just turning red. Soon we entered an austere region of big woods, relieved here and there by rough-looking farms. Scattered through the forest were speckled patches of old snow.

Pushing on, we lost the Red Sox game on the radio. Then we lost reception altogether. We noticed that as the season retreated from spring to late winter, we seemed to be traveling into an earlier era. We passed a farmer collecting maple sap in a wooden vat on runners pulled by two black-and-white oxen, their horns tipped with gleaming brass balls. In a clearing in the woods, a shaggy horse in a working harness stood near a man stacking pulpwood. We caught the scent of wood smoke from a farmhouse attached to a barn by a ramshackle shed. A bedraggled wreath adorned the boarded-up front door. Some of the barns and sheds were decorated with rural scenes that could have been inspired by the poetry of Robert Frost. Who, we wondered, had painted them? A school bus from the '40s, converted to a hunting camp, with a set of deer antlers over the cracked windshield, slumped in a clearing. We passed mailboxes with the names Desjardins, Thibeau, Lafleur, and Lanoue lettered on them. Had we blundered over the border into Canada?

7
THE CHRISTLY KINGDOM

We arrived in Orleans around six that evening. The town consisted of a furniture factory across the river from several gray row houses; a main street lined with storefronts reminiscent of those in a nineteenth-century prairie town; a single railroad track; a squat brick bank; and a white, three-story wooden hotel. On an abandoned siding near the river sat an ancient Great Northern boxcar. Some wag — perhaps one of our prospective students — had painstakingly inscribed, in bold capital letters, the word EXPRESS on the side of the boxcar: Great Northern Express. Somewhere, we trusted, there was a high school.

There was no traffic at all, so I stopped in the street to consult the hand-drawn map that the superintendent of schools had sent us. As we studied the map, two men wearing red wool jackets, wool pants, and muddy lumbering boots came staggering out of the hotel, apparently engaged in a fistfight. The combatants were too drunk to hurt each other much, but the slugfest raged all over Main Street. Grappling for advantage, they crashed into the grille of my grandparents' Oldsmobile, which we'd borrowed to drive to our interview.

Now — showing how absolutely green in the ways of the world I was, how sopping wet behind the ears — I rolled down my window and called out to those two lugs, in all seriousness, "Excuse me. Could one of you gentlemen please tell us how to get to the high school?"

"Well, hell, we can do better than that," the taller one said. "We can *take* you there."

Whereupon, without invitation, the pugilists piled into the backseat of Gramp's Olds, bearing more than a whiff of damp wool, evergreen pitch, chain-saw gas, and beer. But there was another scent in the air, one I'd been vaguely aware of since our arrival in Orleans, a sweetish odor that seemed familiar, though I couldn't quite identify it.

"Hang a Christly right at the hotel," the tall brawler shouted in my ear.

I hung a right. After several more abrupt turns, mostly into private driveways that our inebriated guides had mistaken for public thoroughfares, we pulled up in front of a

33

small brick school building. The back doors of the car opened and our benefactors poured themselves out. Waving off my thanks, they weaved up the middle of the street, arms around each other's shoulders like two affectionate school chums. But as I turned into the parking lot, I glanced back and saw them shoving each other. The smaller man threw a wild haymaker, and they were at it again. "Well, sweetie," Phillis said as we headed up the granite steps of the school for our interview, "welcome to the Christly Northeast Kingdom."

The superintendent — "Just call me Prof" — made a strong pitch. The classes were small, and the students, he assured us, were farm and small-town kids, unsophisticated but hard-working and bright, who did not want to go directly from high school into the local furniture factory. Above all, Prof told us, our job would be to "keep the kids out of the mill." Admittedly, the salaries were abysmal: $4,100 for a beginning male teacher, $3,900 for a woman. Incredibly, in many Vermont schools in those days, men were routinely paid more on the assumption that most women would leave the classroom after a few years to have children — and thus were worth less. Prof allowed that even though the salary schedule was discriminatory, he'd had no luck getting the school board to change the policy. A broad-shouldered former English teacher and coach, now in his fifties, with a big, red, earnest face and a loud voice, the superintendent shrugged. You fight the battles you have some chance of winning, he told us.

To be sure, a heavy redolence of fermented grain mash hung about the stocky old educator. Could it be that everyone in this boreal enclave was an alcoholic? I supposed that Prof had just finished dinner and had had a couple of drinks with his meal — and his personal habits weren't our business, anyway.

We'd come prepared to be quizzed about our college classes and grades, educational philosophies, extracurricular activities, and how long we intended to stay in the area. None of those subjects came up. It quickly became apparent that Prof was desperate to find two warm bodies to fill the science and English vacancies at Orleans High School. He did inquire whether we thought we could make the kids behave. "I'll just tell you one thing on that score," he said. "If you have to knock 'em down, make sure they stay down. That includes my two boys, Big Prof and Little Prof. They're the worst

35

of the lot. Do you have any questions?"

The only query we could think of was how the Northeast Kingdom had gotten its name. Happy to be back on safe ground, Prof explained that the Kingdom was usually considered to comprise the three northeasternmost counties of Vermont: Orleans, Caledonia, and Essex. As for its name, during the 1950s, the then-governor of Vermont, George Aiken, had coined it in recognition of the region's rugged beauty.

To clinch the deal, having learned that we both liked to fish, Prof walked us down School Street to the Willoughby River and showed us, in the April dusk, the very large rainbow trout leaping the falls on their way upriver to their spring spawning beds. The jumping trout did the trick. Back in the superintendent's office, we signed our contracts on the spot.

Not until we walked out to my grandparents' car, however, did I recognize that pervasive aroma I'd noticed earlier. Then I understood my deeper affinity for this remote northern mill town and the mountains surrounding it. The scent of varnish from the furniture factory was identical to that in the air of my hometown in the Catskills when the woodworking factory was open. Like the odors of sawdust, lumber seasoning in the open air, evergreen woods, and the cold river where Prof had taken us to see the leaping trout, the fragrance of varnish was, to me, the scent of a potential home.

8
A Run of Hard Luck

It was the dawn of June 2, my sixty-fifth birthday, and the Loser Cruiser and I were headed east out of town on the first leg of the Great American Book Tour. In the rear-view mirror, I could see Phillis waving from our front porch. Suddenly, I found myself remembering my first day of high school. We'd just moved again to the tiny, rural village of Cato, in the snow belt of central New York, where my dad had recently been appointed superintendent of schools. I was sitting in my homeroom when I looked up and noticed, coming through the door, arms laden with books, a pretty, slender strawberry blonde with the sweetest smile I'd ever seen.

I soon learned that Phillis was the kindest, smartest, funniest girl in my new school. We began sitting next to each other in our classes, and my early adolescent attempts at fiction were satirical portraits of our teachers written solely to amuse her. Later, when we began dating seriously, our romance had a delicious and, to us, mostly hilarious Capulet-Montague flavor, since Phillis's mother was suing a politically controversial teacher my dad firmly supported, and our families were arch enemies. For a year or so, Phillis and I had to meet on the sly, stealing passionate kisses and laughing ourselves silly behind the walnut tree in her front yard. Today, however, these recollections threatened to derail me before I was out of sight of home. Ten seconds into my journey, I missed the light and love of my life so badly I could have burst into tears.

"Get a grip on yourself, Howard Frank," Reg said. He was sitting beside the front passenger-side door in what, from that moment on, I would think of as the catbird seat. "This was your idea, remember? A book tour is Murphy's Law writ large. My advice is to brace yourself."

My uncle, the realist, was right. Over the next two weeks, during my New England "saturation tour," I

1. Received an e-mail in Blue Hill, Maine, from my publisher, informing me that the first national review of my new book had trashed it as a

prime example of "storytelling run amok."

2. Learned in Boston that there'd been a good review of my novel in *Publishers Weekly*. "Too late," said the gleeful critic in my head. "But look at it this way, Harold. Who wants to read something good about an author, anyway?"

3. Was rebuked by a well-fed gentleman in a clerical collar in Northhampton, Massachusetts, for "contributing to the addictions of panhandlers," because I slipped a buck to a young man with a cardboard sign reading HOMELESS AND HUNGRY. That same day the gas tank fell off the Loser Cruiser in Portland, and I had to bum a ride to my downtown event in a commercial bread truck.

All in all, the Great American Book Tour was off to a shaky start.

9
MORE WOES OF
A TOURING WRITER

The chain bookstore, not far from Boston, was located in a large mall, the sort where you can buy everything under the sun and nothing that any sensible member of our species could conceivably need or might actually want. I could find only one vacant parking space — right in front of the bookstore, as it happened. And glory be, as I heaved down upon it in the clanking old Loser Cruiser, hunkered behind the steering wheel in my ancient Red Sox jacket and cap, the once red "B" above the bill long since faded to the same rusty hue as my car, right in the middle of the parking slot I spotted a stand-alone sign: AUTHOR'S EVENT TODAY. THIS SPACE RESERVED FOR HOWARD FRANK MOSHER.

Leaving the Cruiser running — the remnants of the wired-on exhaust system sounded as loud as a jet engine through the crevasse in the floor under the brake pedal

41

— I got out to move the sign.

Out from the big-box store, at a purposeful clip, came a young gentleman in a black suit, black necktie, and highly polished black shoes. Around his neck hung an ID badge proclaiming him to be the manager. Good Jesus! The guy was a dead ringer for a painting I'd seen recently of Genghis Khan in his twenties.

"Hey!" he called out. "That sign is there for a reason."

"What's the reason?" I said.

"Read the sign. We've got an author coming this afternoon. That place is reserved."

I pretended to study the sign. "I'll get right out of here," I said.

"Well, you'd better," said the Scourge of the Steppes. "Can't you read?"

I hopped back into my thundering car, pulled out of my designated parking spot, flashed the chain-store manager a thumbs-up, and drove around behind the mall, parking beside a large green Dumpster.

"I'm not telling you what to do, Howard," said Uncle Reg. "But I can tell you what *I'd* do in this situation."

I was sure I knew exactly what he would do in this situation, and it would not be pretty. Then again, I wasn't my uncle. I removed my baseball cap and jacket and

42

made my way on foot around to the front of the store, where the child Genghis was worriedly looking at his watch.

"He isn't here yet?" I said. "Your author?"

The guy shook his head. "Sometimes they don't show up at all. You wouldn't believe how high-handed some of these writers are."

I realized that not only did my corporate friend not recognize me as his author — he hadn't even connected me with the poor apparitional dummy in the Loser Cruiser.

I gave him a reassuring pat on the shoulder. "I imagine your writer will be here any minute," I said, and headed in to do my event at the first and last chain bookstore on my itinerary. This was starting to be fun, and I wasn't even out of New England yet.

10

AN INAUSPICIOUS BEGINNING

Queequeg was a native of Kokovoko, an island far away to the West and South. It is not known on any map; true places never are.
— HERMAN MELVILLE, *MOBY-DICK*

I paused and peered over my teacher's copy of *Moby-Dick* at twenty bewildered students. "What do you think Herman Melville means when he writes that true places can't be found on a map?"

?

Then, from Bill, who I'd been told was something of a teenage genius, "What do *you* think he means, Mr. Mosher?"

Aha! The night before, preparing my first-ever set of teaching lessons, I had underlined the phrase "true places" and had written in the margin, "Discuss!" Not six months earlier, my own American literature professor had explicated this grand and mysterious passage, which had stimulated all kinds of compelling — and certainly a few not so compelling — discussions in lit courses, graduate-level seminars, and Great Books reading groups. Fifteen seconds into my new profession, here was my chance to shine. Thank you, Bill.

There was just one problem. At the moment, I couldn't recall a single word of what my professor had said about *Moby-Dick* or any other book. Truth to tell, I didn't have the faintest notion what Herman Melville was talking about. What's more, it was on the tip of my tongue to say so. At least I might get a laugh out of these solemn Vermont kids.

Then came salvation. Sort of.

"Mr. Mosher?"

"Yes, Bill?"

"You know Cody? The kid you loaned your car to right before class? Who said he had an emergency at home?"

"Yes?"

This yes was more tentative. Already I was wondering how I could have done anything so dumb. Tossing my car keys to a kid who, just as Bill had been lauded as the class star, had been pointed out to me as a born troublemaker.

Bill craned his neck to look out the window. "He's driving by the school in your station wagon at about sixty miles an hour."

"Jesus Christ!" I shouted, running to the window to see. The whole class was up and making for the window.

As I stumbled over a desk, Bill, peering down onto School Street, nodded admiringly and said, "In reverse."

11
AN ENCOUNTER

Moose can be aggressive any time,
especially in early summer when a cow
feels her very young calf is in danger.
A charging moose often kicks forward
with its front feet, knocking down
the threat, then stomping and kicking
with all four feet.
— WASHINGTON STATE
DEPARTMENT OF FISH AND WILDLIFE

Some forty-three years later, posting toward my last New England event before heading, like Melville's Ishmael, into uncharted waters, I had to admit that the first weeks of my trip had not been an unqualified success. True, I had signed, and even sold, a fair number of books. All over New England, I had met some of the most knowledgeable and dedicated independent booksellers anywhere. They were not only keeping writers like Harold Who going, but

47

they very well might be keeping "the book" itself, as we knew it, alive. At the same time, I had lost a gas tank, been pilloried as a madman in an important early review, and kicked the hell out of my own parking space at a bookstore that looked like a Walmart. I couldn't help wondering whether any other MacArthur recipient had gotten a fellowship period off to such an unpropitious start.

Encouragingly, my event that evening in Vermont at the excellent Norwich Bookstore was standing room only, and I had a whole day to get to my next engagement, in New York City. Why not celebrate the end of my saturation tour of New England by treating myself to a cholesterol-saturated breakfast at the McDonald's in White River Junction? Defiantly, I ordered a bacon, egg, and cheese biscuit and a large cup of Newman's Own with two creams, to go. Breakfast in hand, I started back across the vacant lot separating the restaurant from the Comfort Inn — a misnomer if there ever was one — where I'd bivouacked the night before. As I dawdled along, nattering pleasantly to my many invisible friends, a large bus painted a violent lavender hue and adorned with foot-high scarlet Chinese characters pulled up to the entrance of the motel. Fifty or so tourists with luggage milled around, preparing to board the bus for a day of sightseeing.

At that moment, out of the June mist hanging over the lot stepped a gigantic cow moose, with a wobbly spring calf in tow. The mama moose gave a displeased snort. Harold Who stood stock-still, looking at her over his steaming coffee.

"Hello, moose."

This salutation did not cut much ice with Madame *L'orignal,* as the early French explorers named our good friend the North American moose. She snorted again, louder this time. Except for the low, burbling sound of the idling lavender bus and the whining of the long-distance semis on I-91, a few hundred yards away, this little tableau of me, moose, and tourists was unfolding in complete silence. The mother animal began angling my way.

I edged backward. But now the moose-child took it into its outsized head to get between me and the McDonald's, cutting off my only avenue of retreat from the increasingly agitated *mère.* When it comes to *l'orignals,* one never wishes to be in this particular situation: trapped between mother and offspring. In the meantime, some of the Chinese tourists had begun videotaping this bucolic Vermont scene.

The toddler gamboled a few steps toward me. On came its mother, not gamboling. I took a last gulp of Newman's shade-grown java and held out my half-consumed biscuit toward the angry adult animal, now pawing the daisies and paintbrush in the meadow.

Aging Writer Killed by Alarmed Ungulate
Would-be "Touring" Novelist Meets
  Quietus Outside McDonald's
Vermont Elder Caught on Film Being
  Trampled

I put my head down and made a break for the motel. Some of the tourists applauded as I sprinted past the bus. Others were busy filming my dash for life. Glancing over my shoulder, I was relieved to see the moose mother and her child galumphing off toward the scrubby woods at the far edge of the field.

"I see it all from right here," the ancient desk clerk said. "You shouldn't fool with them animals."

"I wasn't fooling with them. I was trying to get away from them."

Some of the tourists had drifted back inside the lobby. A smiling young man began videoing the exchange between me and the clerk.

"He trying to get away," the cameraman said, staunchly taking up my part. "Trying to get away from big deer small deer."

"You're lucky to be alive, bud," the clerk told me.

"Very fortunate to be alive," the Beijing filmmaker agreed.

One of his compatriots said something in Chinese. "He ask, what you do for work," my videotaping friend said.

"I'm a writer. On a book tour."

My interlocutor turned to our growing gallery and translated my reply. The man who had inquired about my occupation said something funny. At least I judged it was funny because several of the other tourists laughed.

"He say," my personal translator told me, "now you go hotel room write all about being chase by big deer small deer."

Whereupon the desk clerk favored me with a baleful grin.

"No," I said, "I don't think so. I think that now I'm going to get in my car and head straight home. End of the book tour. End of the writing career. QED. Time to go fishing."

In the event, of course, it wasn't that easy. After more good-natured laughing, photo opportunities, and handshaking all around,

51
SAYVILLE LIBRARY

after returning to my room and showering and shaving, after checking out of the goddamn Comfort Inn in White River Junction, I discovered, somewhat to my relief, that the Loser Cruiser simply refused to take me home.

As the Cruiser and I huffed, chuffed, and, every time we hit 58.5 miles an hour, shimmied our way south, I was ashamed of my wavering. Rejuvenated, I stopped at a rest area outside Albany and jotted down the following lines, my first ever attempt at something like haiku:

Big deer small deer chase
Vermont writer born under
Sign of jackass.

"Not bad for a beginner," I said after reading my haiku aloud to my uncle in the catbird seat.

"Stick to fiction," he said. "Let's roll the wagons."

12
CHICHESTER

Heading south on the New York State Thruway toward my evening engagement in New York City, I found myself glancing off to the west at the hazy blue Catskills and thinking again of my hometown and its chronicler, my uncle Reginald Bennett. A trim, athletic man with dark hair and the brightest china-blue eyes I've ever seen, Reg grew up in Chichester and worked at the factory as a young man. Though he never attended high school, he began teaching at the village's one-room school when he was sixteen. Years later he put himself through college and graduate school at Albany State — now SUNY Albany — and became the local superintendent of schools, with a couple of dozen tiny mountain schoolhouses to visit and staff. In the early 1950s he led a lengthy, acrimonious battle for regionalization and was the driving force behind the Onteora Central School. On several occasions his life was threatened by opponents of the new school. Once, in a Phoenicia grocery store, he defended himself against a belligerent taxpayer with the nearest weapon at hand — a can of corn!

In fact, Reg Bennett was much loved in Chichester and beyond as a man of unswerving integrity, wry humor, and profound generosity. He was meticulous in every aspect of his life, from his dress and appearance to the way he transplanted a white birch tree or a yellow rosebush or introduced a particularly colorful river stone to his rock garden. A wide and deep reader, his favorite novelists were the elegant, hardboiled detective writers Dashiell Hammett and Raymond Chandler; he also loved the lyrical prose of Hemingway and Fitzgerald, whom he affectionately referred to as Hem and Scott, as if they were neighbors or old fishing friends. His extensive private library included first editions of *The Sun Also Rises, The Great Gatsby,* and Thomas Wolfe's *You Can't Go Home Again* — a phrase he loved to cite because, after a stint in the navy, he'd made his own journey home and stayed there. He revered Ty Cobb and Ted Williams, renowned scrappers, like the mountain folks who made their way into his unpublished history of Chichester, *The*

Mountains Look Down. Sadly, when Reg died, his Chichester memoir went missing. Its mysterious disappearance was one of the keenest disappointments of my life.

Suddenly I had an idea. It seemed highly unlikely that I would ever locate the missing Chichester manuscript — I'd searched for it for a decade and a half with no luck — but why not slope over to the Catskills this afternoon and revisit my hometown? Like the Sabbath and mankind in the parable, book tours were made for authors, I told myself, not the other way around. Which is how, an hour later, I found myself standing beside the little stream high on the mountainside where my father and uncle and I had once gone to listen to the Yankee–Red Sox games, looking down at the town where I'd been born.

"Tell me a story," I mused out loud to my road-bud uncle.

"I'll tell you a story," said a sharp female voice. "You're trespassing. I want you and that — that *vehicle* of yours — off my property immediately."

Good heavens! The woman glaring down from the bank above bore a fearsome resemblance to my junior-high English teacher, Mrs. Earla "Battle-ax" Armstrong. Could she possibly be the long-deceased Battle-ax, come back from the other side to give me one more comeuppance? This woman was wearing expensive hiking shoes and wielding a hefty blackthorn walking stick. Otherwise, the likeness was uncanny.

"How many more of you are down there?" the Battle-ax said.

"More of me?"

"Who were you talking to a minute ago?"

"Oh, that was just — me."

Trespassing Author Receives Drubbing Within Sight of Ancestral Home

I couldn't help myself. Just like my smart-aleck twelve-year-old self back in Mrs. Armstrong's class, I began to laugh.

"What's so funny?" said the indignant landowner.

"I'm sorry," I told her, clambering up the bank. "I caught my first trout right here when I was four. This is where my uncle and dad and I used to come to listen to ball-games on the car radio."

At this point I think "Mrs. Armstrong" realized that, whoever or whatever I might be, I was relatively harmless. A calculating tone crept into her voice as she said, "Actually, I'm not around all the time. I live in New

56

York City. I'll tell you what," she continued. "You're welcome to fish up here if you'll keep an eye on my property. You know, notify me if you see anybody suspicious-looking."

By then, however, I was hotfooting it back to the Loser Cruiser. Ten seconds later I was bouncing down the old logging road and waving out the window to the Battle-ax.

Yet as I drove back over to the Thruway, leaving the tiny mountain hamlet I'd left behind all those years ago, I knew I was taking along some unfinished business.

13
NEW YORK

It is a truth universally acknowledged, or if it isn't it should be, that lighting out on a road trip is almost never the wrong thing to do. The Blackfoot Indians knew this back when the only roads were buffalo trails. They had plenty of bison to hunt right in their own backyard, but frequently they would range over hundreds and even thousands of miles just to see what they could see. We hardly ever regret a road trip, and on the best ones, no matter the vicissitudes of the highway, the times, our age or career or health, there comes a moment when we know that it was *exactly* the right thing to do.

For me, on the Great American Book Tour, that moment came in about as unlikely a place as I can imagine. Late in the afternoon on the hazy June day when I was harried out of my hometown by the Battle-ax, I found myself traipsing from bookstore to bookstore in New York City. I was thinking of what my uncle and I had planned to do here — visit the great writer Joe Mitchell's beloved fish markets, have a look at the Battery, immortalized by Herman Melville in *Moby-Dick* — when I stopped in my tracks in the middle of Fifth Avenue. Surrounded by honking delivery trucks, street vendors, tourists, homeless people, and fans in Derek Jeter sweatshirts hustling to catch the subway out to the stadium for that night's Yankee game, I stood stock-still. Staring at me from less than one hundred feet away crouched the two lions I'd first seen as a boy of six, holding my uncle's hand and wondering if they were getting ready to spring. Not that I was all that worried. If the big cats attacked, I had no doubt that Reg could handle them, just as he had that assailant in the grocery store, whom he'd beaned with the can of corn.

"Get out of the way, Clyde, you're not home in East Jesus," a cab driver screeched as he swerved around me.

I did as he said. Then stood on one of the busiest sidewalks in America, looking at those lions. And right then, I knew that setting out on this improbable journey, at this fraught juncture of my life, had been exactly the right decision.

■ ■ ■ ■

I have to confess that I'm no fan of misogynistic old Paul (formerly Saul). I've always suspected that on the road to Damascus, he was either falling-down drunk or struck by lightning. How else to account for his promptly going out and inventing a new religion that would consign me, for the better part of my youth, to that exquisitely cruel inner circle of Hades known as Sunday school? Still, personal epiphanies do happen. I experienced a small one in front of the main branch of the New York Public Library that day. And I'm pretty sure I'd had another one, many years before.

On the day of our wedding, Phillis and I drove from upstate New York to the Northeast Kingdom, just as we had done in the spring for our teaching interview. We arrived in Orleans around midnight, but Verna, our new landlady and soon to be our dear friend, was waiting up for us. "Welcome home, Moshers!" she called out as we approached her lighted porch. "Welcome home."

Until that moment we'd had doubts, and plenty of them, about deciding to come to this little outpost a few miles south of the

Canadian border to start our married life. With her simple, warm greeting, Verna laid those doubts to rest. Whatever lay ahead for us, we knew that at least for the next year, this was the place we would call home.

14
THE BAD BOY
AND THE BATTLE-AX

Phillis was loyally waiting for me outside Prof's office at six o'clock on the evening of my less-than-triumphant first day as a teacher at Orleans High School. That's when the red-faced old superintendent finally finished explaining to me why lending my car to a bona fide juvenile delinquent and taking the name of the Lord in vain at the top of my lungs in front of my senior English class were pedagogically unsound decisions. Prof told me that in all his years in the school business, "No damn fool of a first-year teacher ever got off to a worse start than Howard Mosher."

Well. Like Phillis, I was teaching six classes and supervising two study halls and a shift of lunch duty. I was coaching various sports and directing student plays. Not to mention advising the senior class, which would entail writing multiple college or job recommendations for thirty or so kids. We'd received dinner invitations to the homes of students and offers to take us fishing and hunting. Despite my blasphemous outburst on that first day of school, the officials of the United Church of Orleans beseeched us both to teach Sunday school. "Just be sure to buy your beer in the next town over," Prof said when I told him the news.

My problem wasn't that I did not like teaching, which I did, or even that I wasn't very good at it, which I wasn't. My main concern was that I didn't have an hour of time for my writing. Maybe that's just as well. At twenty-one I wasn't ready to write the stories of the Northeast Kingdom. But I was more than eager to hear them, and as those busy early weeks in our new home raced along, it soon became obvious that in the Kingdom we had discovered a mother lode of stories. Our landlady, Verna, a twice-widowed woman in her late sixties, had lived most of her life on a Kingdom hill farm. The morning after we moved in, she invited us downstairs to her apartment for coffee with several elderly neighbors. "These are the Moshers, Howard and Phillis," Verna announced. "They got married yesterday in New York State and drove clear up here to Vermont to go to bed together."

One evening not long after we arrived,

Verna told us how, during the Depression, she had saved her farm by manufacturing and selling moonshine. Years later she married the revenue agent who had caught her red-handed but declined to arrest her because he knew she'd lose her home if he did. When Verna finished her story, I looked across the kitchen table at Phillis, and she looked back at me. Neither of us spoke. But I knew, and Phillis knew, not only that I *wanted* to write stories about the Northeast Kingdom, but that one way or another, I was *going* to write them.

First, though, I had to learn something about teaching, and quickly.

Phillis was a well-trained science teacher. She knew how to prepare interesting lessons, set up labs, devise fair tests. I was an aspiring storyteller who did not know jack. "Read aloud to the kids, a little every day," Prof suggested. "Even high school kids love to be read to. Read them something they wouldn't be apt to read on their own. Dickens, Frost. They'll love it."

Under his desk Prof kept several quarts of Budweiser. He assessed his school days according to whether they were one-quart or two-quart days. A two-quart day was a bad one. "This is number three," he said the day he advised me to read aloud to my students.

As the fall progressed, I discovered that not only did the kids I taught like to be read to. They wanted me to *tell* them stories, especially from my boyhood in the Catskills. For survival purposes, I bribed them. Two stories a day, one at the beginning of class, the other at the end, *if* they turned in their homework on time and did their outside reading. For their listening pleasure I invented a character I called the Bad Boy of Chichester, whose life and times we followed from one misadventure to the next. The Bad Boy was a composite of several rapscallions I had hobnobbed with as a kid, mixed with a great deal of my own personal history. Of my many Bad Boy of Chichester stories, my students' favorite was "The Bad Boy and the Battle-ax." The kids begged me to tell it at least once a week.

Now, my aforementioned junior-high English teacher, Mrs. Earla Armstrong, aka the Battle-ax, hated kids. Not just some kids — all kids, everywhere. It was confidently retailed in the Chichester of my boyhood that there was never a child Mrs. Armstrong did not despise. Her favorite prediction was that not one of us would "amount to a hill of beans."

65

"Look here, Mosher," she said one day when she apprehended me writing a Wild West outlaw tale instead of starting my homework. "If you want to write stories, you have to do three things. Read the classics. Revise your work. Write what you know. But even if you do," she added with delphic certitude, "I very much doubt that you'll ever amount to a hill of beans." With this happy prophecy, she tore my little attempt at a Western to shreds and threw it in the wastepaper basket.

To which I replied, "Thank you, Battle-ax."

A dreadful silence ensued as Mrs. A, who had a cruel flair for the dramatic, let that "Battle-ax" hang on the dusty air of the classroom. Then she nodded grimly, marched back to the Bad Boy's desk, and, without breaking stride, belted him smack upside of the head with her big, hard, meaty hand, knocking him clean out of his seat onto the floor. Seeing many fine constellations never viewed by any astronomer, ancient or modern, the Bad Boy of Chichester struggled to his feet, slumped into his chair, and raised his hand.

"What now?" she said.

"Thank you, Battle-ax," I said again, to the horror of everyone, most of all myself.

"I deserved that."

And I will be damned if the old buzzard didn't hammer me again, knocking me into the *other* aisle.

Two quick footnotes. When I complained about Mrs. Armstrong to my father, by then the school principal, he readily agreed that she was a battle-ax but suggested I not call her one to her face again. Many years later, when I resurrected Mrs. A as the draconian schoolteacher in my novel *Northern Borders,* she was the only real person I ever used in a work of fiction without changing her name. I don't think I did this for spite. By then Mrs. Armstrong had long since been recruited to lord it over some unruly classroom in the celestial beyond. The truth is that I simply could not think of my fictional schoolteacher-character as anyone other than Earla Armstrong, whose advice to me about writing stories remains, to this day, the best I have ever received: "Read the classics. Revise your work. Write what you know."

What else can I say? Thank you, Battle-ax.

15
WASHINGTON, D.C.

The novel I'd been searching for over the past thirty years certainly wasn't a classic. Not, at least, in the sense that Mrs. Earla Armstrong had meant. (Mrs. A read *Pride and Prejudice* and *Emma* at her desk during lunch hour while sipping coffee laced with gin out of an enormous black thermos.) The book I was looking for was a comic novel about a Canadian con man, set during World War I and the Great Depression. I'd loved it, just roared over page after page, but I had loaned it to my mother-in-law, who loaned it to a schoolteacher friend, who passed it along to someone else, and *do* you think that I could remember either the title or the author? My search for that damn novel had, over the years, turned into a quest, and if every journey is to some extent informed by a private agenda quite different from its stated purpose, my private agenda on the Great American Book Tour was to find that con-man story.

What better places to look than the great independent bookstores I was visiting, sometimes several a day? Not that I really expected to find the book. The search had become an end in itself, a perfect excuse to haunt the fiction sections of bookstores, new and used, and libraries, small and large. While I love to write, and can do so almost anywhere and under almost any circumstances, like many other writers of my acquaintance, I live to read. There's no place I'd rather hang out than a bookstore or library.

I didn't find the con-man novel in the extensive fiction section of 192 Books in New York City, where I had a terrific event on the evening after my visit to the Catskills. Or in the public library on Fifth Avenue, where the marble lions kept their own counsel and were of no help to me at all. Nobody at Chester County Book and Music, the wonderful indie on the western outskirts of Philadelphia, had heard of it, though my bookseller friend Michael Fortney suggested that after I got home from my tour, I should send a summary of the story to the book-search Web site ABE.com and see what I could find out.

No luck at Baltimore's fine Ivy Bookshop

or at the world-famous Politics and Prose Bookstore and Coffeehouse in Washington. Just good, lively book discussions at every indie on my itinerary, and several copies of my latest book sold at each store. Right now I was walking along the dusky side streets of Washington, trying to remember where I'd left the Loser Cruiser, when, hello, what's this? In the gutter near a speed bump, I noticed a green Vermont license plate: my own. Evidently the plate had fallen off earlier that evening.

Nearby a tow truck was bellying up to my ancient Chevy. Two burly men with shaved heads, resembling nothing so much as a World Wrestling Federation tag team, got out and eyed the Cruiser. "There's hardly enough left of her to hook onto," one of them remarked.

"Excuse me," I called out. "That's my car. Is it parked illegally?"

"It's abandoned illegally," the larger tag team member said. "No license plate."

I waved the battered plate I'd salvaged from the gutter. "It fell off. Back up the street."

The guys continued to search for a place sufficiently rust-free to attach the tow hook.

"For God's sake," I said. "I'm a novelist from Vermont. Out on a book tour. I've been signing books at the store around the corner."

And I will be hornswoggled if the head WWF brother didn't unhook my car, straighten up, grin at me, and say, "Oh, Politics and Prose? Why didn't you say so? My wife and I buy all our books there. Have for years. What's the name of yours?"

16
RESCUE MISSION IN THE LAND OF THE BLUE AND THE GRAY

The following morning, on the pretext of doing research for his Civil War novel-in-progress, Harold Who drove over to the Manassas National Battlefield Park at Bull Run. Where, almost a century and a half ago, his great-great-great-grandfather, one Padraig Mosher, fresh from County Cork and newly enlisted in the preening New York Zouaves, took to his heels at the first volley, leaped Bull Run Creek in a single bound, and skedaddled back to Washington in record time.

I drove around the battlefield with an eye out for anything that might work its way into my story. Should my Vermont hero come this way? Should he participate in the Battle of Bull Run? Catch a glimpse of fiery old Stonewall harrying my fleet-footed ancestor back to the Union capital? On that sunny June morning nothing jumped out at me as potential material. Until, that is, I approached the creek my forebear reportedly had vaulted — a feat no gazelle could accomplish — and noticed a dozen or so cars backed up before the bridge. Was this a historical reenactment? I detest historical reenactments.

On the bridge, basking in the sunshine, sat a monstrous snapping turtle.

"Go ahead," said my uncle. "Show these city slickers how to handle this situation."

I got out of the car and walked up to the reptile, which must have weighed a good thirty-five pounds. She was covered with moss and creek scum and had wise, courageous, no-nonsense eyes. "Good morning, turtle," I said.

Mrs. Snapper was unimpressed. So unimpressed that she opened her cotton-white mouth and gave out a hiss like a steam kettle. I sprang back, in the grand old tradition of Grandpa Padraig, to considerable laughter from the occupants of the nearby cars.

Approaching the turtle again, I distracted her with my left hand and, as I'd seen my uncle do any number of times, lifted her by the tail with my right hand. Holding her well away from my legs, I started off down the bank toward a sandy little spit along the creek.

I don't know if you've ever tried to pick up an irascible snapper weighing thirty-five pounds, hold the thing out so it can't take a fist-sized chunk of your calf, and walk a hundred feet with it. But suddenly, from a Hummer on the bridge, came a woman's angry voice. "Put that animal down. I'm going to report you on my cell phone to the Humane Society."

Oh, gladly, madam, gladly. Gingerly, I released the now-furious snapper on the nice warm sand beside the stream and started back toward my car. Why were the spectators laughing and honking their horns? They were laughing and honking because, posting along behind me hell-bent for election, came Mrs. Turtle, determined to get back to the road, where she'd wanted to lay her eggs in the first place.

Once again I distracted her with my left hand. Once again the Samaritan in the Hummer shrieked at me. This time it was something about the SPCA.

I ran, yes, ran with the hissing, snapping, washtub-size turtle — how Reg would have laughed — toward a reedy swale upstream, where I deposited my reptilian friend for better or for worse, then bolted for the Loser Cruiser. Horns, mock applause, more threats from Mrs. Battle-ax Armstrong's sister up on the bridge. Padraig Mosher probably ran faster, spurred on as he was by the Rebel cries. But he was no more relieved to reach the safety of our embattled nation's capital than I was to pile into the Cruiser and move on down the line on my Great American Book Tour.

17
FIVE TIPS FOR
CANCER SURVIVORS

From the start of my trouble,
I made a conscious choice not to open
my file and confront what doctors
believed was the worst.
— REYNOLDS PRICE, *A WHOLE NEW LIFE*

During my just-concluded treatment, I too had chosen not to pore over my X-ray images and medical charts, though what was brave defiance and profound faith in Reynolds Price's case was something closer to terror-stricken denial in mine. Still, I found a certain amount of sneaky self-deception useful, so long as it didn't preclude treating the problem immediately. For instance, information I'd gleaned on the Web from the National Cancer Institute stated that radiation usually makes patients "very tired." How could I possibly set out on a hundred-city book tour in a state of fatigue? No, no, I resolved, I damn well was *not* going to be very tired. Or, if I was, I wasn't going to admit it to myself. As for the "diarrhea and frequent and uncomfortable urination" that the booklet *What You Need to Know about Prostate Cancer* warned I would almost certainly experience, well, I'd deal with it, too — as long as I didn't have to dwell on it.

Toward this end, I found that the following activities kept me from perseverating on my disease during my fellowship period:

1. Writing. Anytime I was writing or just transcribing notes into my journal late at night at a cigarette-scorched Motel 6 desk, I felt exactly like my old, hopeful, precancerous self.
2. Helping others. Another truth universally acknowledged is that writers are as solipsistic a pack of ne'er-do-wells as any on the face of the earth. Prolonged illness merely exacerbates our self-centeredness. Still, throughout my treatment and the book tour, I found that any little kindness I could perform for family, friends, or even total strangers lifted me out of myself.
3. Laughing. It may or may not be the

77

best medicine, but I cannot imagine stopping at every interstate rest area between Irasburg, Vermont, and the Pacific without a good sense of the ridiculous.

4. Driving. *Driving?* How could cajoling the ancient and decrepit Loser Cruiser (whose dash lights and radio had shorted out back in Boston) through the labyrinthine interchanges of New York, Philadelphia, Washington, and Richmond, much less Los Angeles; over the Rockies; across the broiling American Southwest; and through the interminable Dakotas with nothing to do but wonder whether my PSA count would be up when I got back to Vermont in the fall for my first posttreatment checkup — how could spending all that time alone in my falling-apart Chevy Celebrity, with a cockeyed license plate wedged in its rear window, possibly distract me from the forty-four radiation sessions I had just undergone, with the jury still very much out on the results? It's simple. Besides the allure of the open road, which has always raised my spirits

like a lark at break of day, I had the strongest sense that with every mile and every rest area, I was somehow outdistancing the accursed cancer.

A delusion? Absolutely. You can't run away from cancer, any more than you can run away from yourself. But if hard traveling, often hundreds of miles a day, in an automobile that should have been junked years ago, was a palliative to keep me from going crazy with worry, self-pity, and stark terror, it was a good one.

5. Reading and discussing books. Already, a few weeks into my tour, I was astonished by the number of books I had acquired. The backseat of the Cruiser was overflowing with them. (The trunk was permanently jammed shut from an encounter with a ten-foot-high Vermont snowbank several winters before.) Driving south toward Richmond, I could not recall a time, during or immediately after my treatment, when I was unable to attain a measure of serenity, and very often joy, by immersing myself in a good book.

More than any other activity,

reading helped me through my cancer treatment and subsequent recovery. But not *just* reading — talking about the books I was reading as well, mainly with booksellers and their customers. Not once did my prostate cancer so much as cross my mind in any of the nearly two hundred bookstores I visited on my Great American Book Tour.

18
GONE FISHING

One evening on our way back from an afternoon of hunting partridge, I told Prof the "Bad Boy and the Battle-ax" story. A few days earlier I'd expressed to him my frustration over not finding suitable literary subjects for my students to write about. "Well, maybe the old Battle-ax was on to something," he said. "Try getting the kids to write about what they know, as she put it. Their own experiences. Then you can nudge them along to write about the books they're reading."

Prof had thick white hair parted in the middle, like a headmaster from the 1930s. He wore large, square, horn-rimmed glasses perched low on the bridge of his bulbous two-quart-a-day nose. At six feet three (his boys, Big and Little, were an inch or so taller) and with the build of an NFL linebacker, he'd been a standout, three-sport high school and college athlete. His proudest moment was scoring fifty points for Orleans High in a basketball game decades ago. He still officiated at local high school games.

Prof's uniform was an old-fashioned double-breasted suit, a wide, multicolored necktie (in an era of dark, narrow ties), and wingtip shoes. He used Old Spice shaving lotion, which, like the three or four packs of clove-scented gum he chewed every school day, diluted, without entirely masking, the beery redolence that enveloped him and his immediate surroundings after ten o'clock each morning. He had a voice like the foghorn of a Great Lakes steamer and never spoke at a normal level when he could shout. He was spontaneously generous. He genuinely liked and understood kids, pretended to be mad more often than he really was (which was often enough), and — the bottom line — always supported his teachers. That is to say, he could and frequently did holler at us, but he brooked no criticism of his staff or beloved school from anyone else, including the school board members. "Old school" was how he accurately described himself. He'd taught three generations of Orleans students and was, in his own eyes and those of nearly everyone else in town, an icon.

Prof's wise advice to encourage my students to write about their own experiences didn't register with me immediately because, good old Kingdom boy that he was, he drank Scotch out of a flask while he road-hunted, and he carried his double-barreled Remington twelve-gauge business end up on the floor between us, on half-cock at all times. That very afternoon, after what Prof had confided was another three-quart day, we were riding the back lanes looking for partridges dusting themselves, when a grouse flew up into a wild apple tree. Prof frantically reached for the loaded gun, brought the barrel sharply up into my chin, yanked the car off the road under the apple tree, jumped out, and missed the bird by a mile.

"Welcome to the Kingdom, sweetie," Phillis said when I got home. "I'm glad he didn't shoot you."

Teaching may be principally a matter of faith. First you must have faith that what you're doing will make a difference. Then you need to have faith in your students. Finally, there's the little matter of faith in yourself. As a first-year teacher at Orleans High School, mine was beginning to evaporate. How was I going to coax, cajole, threaten, or otherwise elicit some written work from my students? Maybe Prof was right. My students might enjoy writing about their own experiences. But what did they know well enough to write about? What were their stories?

On the morning after my hunting mishap, I loosened my necktie, rubbed my black-and-blue chin, and told my seniors that a writer I admired once remarked that the story people want most to read is one they've never read before. I let this sink in for a moment, then said that the one story *they* could write that no one had ever read was their own. Almost everybody, I continued, had a unique story to tell. I was interested in reading theirs.

It would be gratifying to report that the kids went straight home and wrote stunningly original autobiographical essays, won all kinds of writing awards, and received full-freight scholarships to Ivy League colleges. Nothing of the sort happened. Still, I persisted. In school and out, I spent hours talking with my students and, maybe more important, listening to them, trying to help them discover *their* stories. It was a glacially slow process. Ironically, I was probably the main beneficiary of my students' memoirs when they did begin to trickle in. After all, I was the spy in their midst, looking for stories to write myself. To this day I clearly remember three extraordinary essays and the kids who wrote them. I'll call them Ethan, Becca, and Cody — the young hero who borrowed my car on the first day of school.

Like Cody, Ethan detested school, a sentiment I readily understood. The Bad Boy of Chichester had detested school too, for the same reason as Ethan, who longed to spend all day, every day, hunting and fishing. How Ethan had gotten to be a senior I couldn't imagine. Still, I liked him and wanted him to graduate and "stay out of the mill." Therefore, we worked out a deal. Once a week he'd hand in a composition about fishing. We'd go over it together, and if he happened to reveal the whereabouts of a few of his secret trout brooks, that wouldn't hurt his grade either.

Three days later, Ethan produced a twenty-page opus on angling for rainbow trout at the falls on the Willoughby River, where Phillis and I had marveled at the leaping fish on our first evening in the Kingdom. It was a terrific story. Ernest Hemingway would have enjoyed it. I could *see* those hefty, crimson-sided trout jumping the falls, see Ethan carefully drawing a bead on them, hear the rushing water and the sudden, splitting *crack* of his .270 deer rifle as he fired down into the cataract. The next week he composed a spirited panegyric on the art of spearing wall-eyed pike with a trident made from a hay fork. Brook trout were next on the agenda, a fifty-page epic that made me want to grab my fly rod and head out for the streams on the spot.

At the end of the brook trout essay, Ethan appended this succinct message: "Dear Mr. Mosher, so long, gone fishing, yours, Ethan."

19
TWO WRITING REBELS

"You win some, you lose some," Prof consoled me, bleary-eyed from a multi-quart day, as we dumped a burlap sack of wild apples under his bow-hunting tree stand, in express violation of the Vermont Fish and Game Department's regulation forbidding the baiting of white-tailed deer. "Don't give up on those kids, Mosher."

If Ethan, now making his living by selling perch to local grocery stores, was a hard sell when it came to writing, Becca was tougher yet. She wore neon-red lipstick, had a more accurate jump shot than any guy in the school, and barely disguised her disdain for most of her teachers, especially me, because I was, at best, a mediocre speller and Becca had never misspelled a word in her entire sixteen years. One morning not long after my "write your own story" pep talk, she slogged up to my desk and slammed down several sheets of paper. "Don't read this out loud," she said. "It's personal."

Becca wasn't your shy, retiring type. What could be so personal that she'd care whether I read it out loud or not? Right after class I sat down with her essay, titled "Saturday Afternoon at the Orleans Dump."

"My boyfriend's idea of a romantic date is an afternoon shooting rats at the town dump," she began. What followed was a hilarious account of a bored-to-tears Becca, pegging away at gigantic dump rats with her boyfriend's .22. She went on to write about what people hauled to the dump to discard and what you could deduce about their lives from the things that they threw away — dirty magazines, whiskey bottles, not-so-very-old furniture. She wrote about Punk Johnson, the local dumpkeeper, and the treasures he'd salvaged for his tin shack: an ancient Stromberg Carlson radio that didn't work, an armchair with the stuffing leaking out, a cracked blue flower vase. She ended by writing about the mother bear that had ambled by for a late-afternoon snack with her two cubs. Not only could Becca spell. She could write.

The best student composition I received that year came from the worst-behaved kid. That, of course, was Cody, who lived with his mom and little sister in a rusty house trailer slumped in the woods miles from anywhere. He'd been in and out of reform school for years and had Northeast Kingdom outlaw written all over him. Long hair several years before it became fashionable, a small but fiercely loyal gang of like-minded disciples, a mouth on him you'd have to hear to believe. He called me Teach, and despite the little incident with my station wagon on the first day of school, I liked him from the start.

Cody had a pet raccoon named Budweiser, Bud for short, who followed him around like a dog. Bud would come barreling into our apartment, yank open the refrigerator door, sweep everything off the shelves onto the floor, and bare his sharp white teeth and growl if you tried to interfere. Bud was a very large raccoon, and I doubted he'd had his shots. I didn't interfere.

A year or two before Phillis and I arrived in the Kingdom, Cody and the assistant principal got into it over Cody's sneaking Bud into school. The assistant principal, a former leatherneck, told Cody to back off or else. Cody laughed and decked him.

The only positive thing I ever heard anyone say about this kid was that he was good to his sister. As a toddler, she'd been struck in the head by a heavy wooden swing seat, leaving her with irreversible brain damage. Cody ate lunch with his sister, sat next to her on the bus, and generally looked out for her, more like a father than an older brother. Still, he was the student I worried most about.

As the Thanksgiving break approached, I was desperate to get something — anything — in the way of a written assignment from Cody. Finally, I asked him if he'd ever considered writing about Budweiser. "Teach," he said, "I never considered writing about nothing."

A day or two later, to my surprise, he handed me an essay on old Bud. Cody told how he had found the little guy in the road, trying to nurse from his dead mother. He fed the baby raccoon from a doll's bottle and raised him like a house cat — a thirty-pound house cat with a mean streak. It was a wonderful composition. Next he turned to chronicling his life of crime, an essay that could have landed him back in the reformatory for years. Then Cody wrote about the adults he'd like to beat up. It was a long list.

In early December, Cody announced that he and his mom and sister were moving to New Hampshire. On his last day at Orleans

High, he gave me not a composition but a letter, beginning "Dear Teach." It was about his sister. He described what it would be like to be teased by classmates, behind in school, constantly challenged by simple tasks. He told me how his sister might be able to lead a fairly normal life and what their working mom had sacrificed to nurture that hope. He did not mention himself, though he was probably more responsible than anyone else for his sister's progress in school. It was the best student essay I've ever read, before or since. But Cody's story didn't end there.

Some twenty years later, a tall, distinguished-looking man with a touch of gray in his longish hair showed up at our door. He was wearing a suit and tie, but I recognized him immediately. "I was on my way home from a conference in Montreal," Cody said. "I thought I'd stop by and say hello."

Cody came in — I half expected old Budweiser to shamble through the doorway after him and make straight for the refrigerator — and sat down at the kitchen table. He handed me a card with his name printed on it and, below that, his title. He was the superintendent of a large school system in Rhode Island.

"Well," I said, "how did this happen?"

"After I got out of the service and got my degree, I taught special ed for six years," he said. "I was director of special education services for three years, and I've been superintendent of schools in the same district for the past decade."

"I'm going to put this card up on my refrigerator," I told him.

Cody grinned at me. "Hey, Teach," he said. "Could I borrow your car? I've got a little emergency at home that I need to take care of."

20
UNREMAINDERED IN THE CUMBERLAND GAP

At dawn the morning after my well-attended event at Asheville's Malaprop's Bookstore, I was high in the Cumberland Mountains, making my way west in the general direction of Nashville. Just at sunrise I came upon a black bear, promenading along the top of a stone wall to keep the dew off its big padded feet, with all the aplomb of a seasoned Parisian *boulevardier.* The little sidehill farms and wooded hollows and quick mountain brooks of Kentucky reminded me of the Northeast Kingdom.

Up ahead beside the road, a mountaineer in faded overalls and a dark slouch hat was selling snake-shaped walking sticks out of his dooryard. "Pull in here," said my uncle. "He looks like someone we should meet." The carver showed me his great-granny's bed snake. It looked like an old-fashioned wooden wash stick, about three feet long and three inches wide, flat like a yardstick, with a shallow notch cut in the business end. Over time, granny's bed snake had devolved into a stick for stirring boiled peanuts. But the walking-staff carver remembered his grandmother using it to beat the quilt on his boyhood trundle bed to drive out any blacksnakes that might have dropped out of the rafters of their cabin during the day. If necessary, you could pin down an unwelcome bedfellow with the fork in the stick, then remove it, unharmed, to the outdoors.

I bought a walking stick, a beautiful length of native mahogany in the shape of two intertwined serpents sharing a single head. At fifteen dollars, it was by far the best buy, other than the books I purchased, on my entire tour. Then I bought Phillis a jar of sourwood-blossom honey. "Do you see that clump of snakeweed over there?" the carver said, pointing with the bed snake at a wiry bunch of grass on the edge of his neatly swept dirt dooryard. I nodded.

Well, he told me, two days ago he'd witnessed a battle royal, right here in his yard, between a rattler and a king snake. Every time the rattler struck, the king snake would slither off for a mouthful of immunizing snakeweed to counteract the venom, then return to the fray. Eventually, the storyteller assured me, the king snake strangled its larger adversary and ate it whole.

Was the raconteur storying a credulous Yankee descendant of those dastardly perpetrators of the War of Northern Aggression, as my beloved Georgia son-in-law refers to the Civil War? Who cares? Truth may or may not be stranger than fiction, but as that most accomplished of all American storytellers knew, it surely isn't any truer. He was sitting in the catbird seat of the Loser Cruiser, looking right at home in his impeccable white suit, and of course I recognized him immediately.

"What mainly ails fiction these days," Mark Twain told me, "is that most of you newfangled writers have forgotten how to be entertaining."

Twain lit a cigar. "You modern-day storytellers grouse day and night about your poor sales. And they *are* poor. Do you know why? It's because nine out of ten of you are boring. I ask you. Was Shakespeare ever boring? Was Dickens? Tarnation, son, if I want to be bored, I can go to church."

I laughed, but Mr. Twain was just warming to his subject. "How about the second-greatest yarner of all time? Did Jesus ever spin a story that was anything less than

95

entertaining? Not that he didn't try out a few stretchers from time to time. But they certainly weren't tedious. Runaway spend-thrift sons, friendless women about to be stoned to death, victims of highway robbery sprawled senseless along the pikes. Now *there* was a storyteller. And he liked to bend his elbow at a wedding and laze around in the sun and wet a line like Tom and Huck. No wonder Christianity's so popular. What do the Bible and *Huckleberry Finn* have in common?"

"Not much," I ventured.

"Maybe not," Twain said. "But you aren't apt to find either one in a remainder bin."

21
THE LONG APPRENTICESHIP

With his humorous blue eyes, lightning wit, and love for a story, Uncle Reg reminded me of Mark Twain. Reg loved to travel, yet he was as deeply rooted in his home in the Catskills as Twain was on the Mississippi. As a teenager, I loved to sit up late with my uncle listening to his console-model radio. If we couldn't find a baseball game, we listened to country music on faraway relayed stations with exotic call letters: WSM Nashville, WWVA, from Wheeling, West Virginia — even a faint, crackling station from Lookout Mountain, Tennessee.

My love of country music dates from that era. Patsy Cline, crooning her effortless, throaty "I Fall to Pieces." Heehawing Bob Wills and the Texas Playboys. And, of course, the late, great Hank Williams Sr. All rural America was stunned by Hank's death from a drug overdose on New Year's Day, 1953. Even the nationwide mourning de-

97

cades later when the NASCAR legend Dale Earnhardt Sr. hit the wall at Daytona — WE LOVE YOU, DALE proclaimed handlettered cardboard signs in country dooryards from Alabama to the Northeast Kingdom — did not resonate in the little cafés and road-houses and small-town barrooms of America like the shocking news that Hank Senior, not yet thirty years old, was gone.

My favorite song in those days was Hank's "Kaw-Liga (The Wooden Indian)." As my uncle and I listened to the story of the lovelorn cigar-store chief who fell for the carved maiden "over in the antique store," Reg told me that on our long-planned cross-country road tour, we'd dip down to Nash-ville, look up Kaw-Liga, and get our picture taken with him. Maybe even have a snapshot taken of us standing by the baby-blue Cadillac Hank died in on that fateful New Year's Day. Some years later Country Char-ley Pride would do a better rendition of "Kaw-Liga." But no one ever achieved the same broken-voiced, brokenhearted, atonal authenticity, with that country song or any other, as Hank.

As I drove into the rapidly expanding precincts of Steve Earle's Guitar Town that afternoon, heading for my event at Nash-ville's Davis Kidd Bookstore (now, sadly, defunct), humming a bar from Johnny and June Carter Cash's "Jackson," it occurred to me that all of the country songs I loved best told a story. Many of these stories celebrated the lives and homes of people nobody else cared about. Long-distance truckers. Barroom singers. Coal miners and dirt farmers. Down-and-out rodeo riders and hoboes and death-row prisoners.

Like those country music singers in the fall of 1964, I wanted to tell the stories of the loggers and hill farmers and whiskey-runners and moonshiners of the Northeast Kingdom. Though I didn't fully know it, my long apprenticeship, one that all writers and songwriters must serve, not only to their craft but to their material, had begun.

That fall, Phillis and I took weekend canoe trips down north-flowing rivers through the most spectacular fall foliage on the face of the earth and hiked up Jay Peak (pre–ski resort), where we could look out over the mountains of four states and much of southern Quebec. We explored Victory Bog, a vast area of wild swamps and boreal forests. We lollygagged for a whole day at the Orleans County Fair. For hours we moseyed through cattle barns decorated with fall wildflowers in sap buckets, marveled at the fruit and vegetable displays in

Floral Hall, loitered along the midway to the bright loud carousel music — *I'm off to join the circus.* We happily inhaled the mingled scents of cotton candy, beer, fried food, crushed grass, more beer, manure from the animal barns, exhaust fumes from the spinning rides, and more beer. We loved being in love and together at the fair. As twilight fell and the colored lights on the game booths lit up the dusk like Christmas, we proceeded to the grandstand to watch the Joie Chitwood Hell Drivers. Later we drifted to the far end of the midway, where I ogled the "girls" at the three girlie shows — five or six hard-featured, tired-looking women in slit-sided robes swaying to the brassy loudspeaker music on makeshift stages outside gaudy tents.

"Mosher!" A voice I recognized all too well was hissing my name from the press of men lined up outside the Paris Revue tent.

It was Prof, tricked out in an old raincoat with the collar turned up, a fedora with the brim pulled down, and an outlandish red muffler. He couldn't have called more attention to himself if he'd dressed up in a clown's costume.

"Fall in here, Mosher," the old soldier shouted. "My treat!"

I looked at Phillis. "Go ahead, lover boy,"

she said. "I'll wait outside if it's all the same."

I'm not sure what I expected to see inside the Paris Revue tent at the Orleans County Fair. Some sort of burlesque show, I suppose. What I discovered was a new side of the Kingdom. A seething mob of mostly drunken men had congregated around a platform to engage in oral sex with the "performers." "Don't bite, you old bastard — if you do I'll piss on you or rip off your ears," snarled one of the women. A barker wielding an electric cattle prod hovered nearby to keep the drunks off the stage. A somewhat younger woman, Miss Paris Golightly, stumbled out on the platform. From the crowd came a feral growl.

By degrees, it dawned on me that these poor women were not over-the-hill Las Vegas showgirls but very probably sex slaves, transported from one backwater to another to engage in a kind of barbaric prostitution. Later I would learn that most of the women were addicted to heroin or cocaine and were coerced to perform to support their drug habit. Also, that these girlie shows were what kept the fair running in the black. Earlier that week Prof had relayed to the faculty a complaint from a school board member that some of the young women teachers were wearing their dresses too short. I recognized this sanctimonious old codger in the knot of men pushing up to the platform. Two or three of my older students were there as well.

"Only in the Kingdom," I said to Phillis later that night. "What do you do about something like those shows?"

"Write about them, sweetie," she said. "You tell the truth about what you saw and hope that sooner or later someone will put a stop to them."

So, time being a sneaky old bastard, this afternoon I'm in Nashville, turning into the parking lot of the Davis Kidd Bookstore to talk about my new novel from the old Kingdom.

Just down the street from the bookstore was the Bluebird Café, where so many Nashville singers and songwriters have launched their careers, and where, ten years before, I had first met my old country songwriter friend Durwood. His iron-gray hair flowing down onto his shoulders, a double shot in one fist, a foaming draft beer in the other, he beckoned a young singer over to his table, and said, in a voice as rusty as the trailer hitch of a junked tour bus, "Little girl, when you set down to write them purty songs of yours, remember two things. All the best stories are love stories. And don't *never* hold nothing back."

This summer, Durwood was in the middle of a one-man war. His shotgun row house on the west edge of town sat hard by the main line of the Norfolk Southern Railway. For the past several months, one of the rails behind his house had been working its way loose from the ties. Each time a boxcar passed over the unmoored rail, it banged like a rifle shot. Several times through the day and night, the long freights going by turned the entire neighborhood into a battle-zone firefight — *bam bam bam bam* — for up to ten minutes at a time.

Earlier that week Durwood had decided that enough was enough. As the 7:10 City of New Orleans approached, he leaped out from behind the chinaberry tree in his backyard and peppered the lead engine with a double handful of gravel, like David squaring off against Goliath. I had very much hoped, this evening, to witness a rerun of his performance. Instead, when I arrived, Durwood was on the phone to the Norfolk Southern headquarters in Atlanta. Sotto voce, with his hand over the mouthpiece, he informed me that he did not intend to get off the horn until he reached the company's

CEO. An hour of nonstop shouting later, Durwood hung up with a grim smile. Within twenty minutes, a railroad repair truck was pulling into his driveway.

Nashville is full of singers and musicians who, like Durwood, have persisted almost beyond the point of human endurance. Their persistence and faith were not lost on Harold Who, prodding the Loser Cruiser back to his motel through downtown Music City that night. (Have I mentioned that the shock absorbers were shot?)

No doubt someone had left a light on at my Motel 6 that evening, but like the dash lights on the Cruiser, it seemed to have burned out. Groping in the dark for the doorknob, I began to laugh. It must have been the rinky-dink piano music from the club next door to the motel that reminded me. For the first time in years, I found myself thinking about a battered old piano in a Prohibition-era Northeast Kingdom roadhouse and the chain of events leading to my thirty-year friendship with Jim Hayford.

22
A MUSIC LESSON

Late one afternoon in the fall of 1964, at the glorious peak of the foliage season, with the hills surrounding Orleans solid blocks of polished reds, yellows, and oranges, Prof appeared at our door with his sons, Big and Little Prof, in tow. He informed me that he'd borrowed a farm truck from a school board member to "go fetch Hayford a Christly piano" — a nearly new Baldwin in mint condition, advertised for sale in the local paper by a recently retired teacher in nearby Barton. Jim Hayford, the school's music teacher, was a former student of Robert Frost's and a fine lyric poet in his own right. I will return to Jim presently. In the meantime our superintendent, having had another two-quart day, had stopped by to recruit me to drive the truck. The boys rode in the back, and Prof sat up front with me, working on quart number three.

The owner of the piano wasn't at home

when we arrived, so we poked around in an old carriage shed, looking at some other items for sale: a sleigh with elegant curved iron runners, some wooden maple-sugaring buckets, a crosscut saw, and another piano, this one lidless, with most of its ivories missing and a Rhode Island Red hen nesting in its innards. When the schoolteacher arrived a short while later, she told us that her husband had bought the beat-up piano in the shed for five dollars when an infamous local roadhouse called the Rum Hound closed its doors in the late 1940s. She invited us into her parlor to inspect the Baldwin, upon which Prof played a one-finger, three-quart bar of "Chopsticks." Pronouncing the instrument satisfactory, he wrote a personal check to the teacher, and, with Big and Little rolling their eyes, we manhandled the thing out onto the porch and down two planks into the truck. Prof secured it with a frayed hank of baling twine tied off with a knot he claimed to have learned in the navy during "the war" — a lie so monstrous that Big and Little burst out laughing.

Back in Orleans, Prof had an inspiration. Why not slope over to Cliff Street and surprise old Hayford with the piano before carting it to the school? Instantly I thought of a number of very good reasons why not. Cliff Street had not been idly named; it was as steep as any street in San Francisco. Nor was the truck, whose regular brakes were at best questionable, equipped with a working emergency brake. Riding through Orleans, Prof called out to his fishing cronies on the street, whistled at two miniskirted young secretaries on their way home from the mill, waved his empty quart out the window like a frat boy on an initiation rite.

"Slap her in first gear and gun her, Mosher!" Prof roared, heaving the empty onto the village green, where a contingent of public-spirited church ladies were raking up leaves. "To the bold go the laurels!"

I jammed the shaky floor-shift knob into first and we started up Cliff Street. The bank president was out on his lawn burning leaves, the scent evoking a fleeting memory of Chichester and my uncle. Up the hill, Jim and Helen Hayford's big, yellow, ornately gingerbreaded house came into sight.

We never reached it.

"Stop! We can't hold the piano back," the boys yelled from the truck bed. I mashed down on the worn metal brake pedal with every ounce of my weight. Prof piled out of the cab. Unsurprisingly, the baling twine had parted, and even though Big and Little

Prof were as rugged as any two grown men in town, they were no match for gravity, and that quarter-ton piano was tilted up on the truck bed at a terrifying pitch. Somehow, with Prof's help, they lowered it onto the street. Before they could gee-haw it around at right angles to the hill, it got away from them. Down Cliff Street on its sturdy casters rolled the nearly new Baldwin. Down Cliff Street, running nimbly alongside the fugitive instrument, went Prof and his great big boys.

"T I M — *B E R!*" Prof hollered as the runaway piano hurtled over the riverbank. One of the legs snapped off, then another. The Baldwin flipped onto its lid and kept going. It skidded down the bank and plunged into the rapids where, with a final crescendo, it splintered into kindling.

"I got my piano, Howard," Jim told me the next morning before school. "But it seems to have undergone a transformation. There's a nest of some kind inside it."

I accompanied him downstairs to the music room, where I was amazed to see the battered old roadhouse piano from the former schoolteacher's carriage shed. Evidently, after dropping me off at my apartment, Prof and his boys had returned to

Barton, purchased this old wreck, and, under cover of darkness, brought it to the school. Jim listened gravely as I told him what I guessed had happened.

When I finished, he nodded and tinkled a couple of the remaining upper-register ivories. "I'm reminded," he said, "of what my great-grandfather said to Mark Twain after hearing him speak in Burlington."

"Which was?"

"Mr. Clemens, that was the funniest talk I've ever heard. It was so funny, it was all I could do to keep from laughing."

23
THE DICKENS OF
BEALE STREET

"My name is Franklin Roosevelt Beaufort," the gray-haired, deep-voiced black man said as he bent over the toy computer keyboard. Pecking away at the brightly painted letter keys, he rumbled on: "I was born during the Great Depression in the Mississippi Delta. Over by Greenwood, yeah. My parents were poor but honest sharecroppers. When I was six years old, my daddy left home. Oh, yeah. That summer I began work in the cotton fields 'longside my mama . . ."

It was five in the morning, and I was sipping very hot, very strong coffee in a café on Memphis's Beale Street. Down the block someone was picking out, over and over, the first few bars of Scott Joplin's "The Entertainer." Otherwise, on this summery dawn, the blues capital of the upper Delta was as quiet as it ever would be.

Inside the café Franklin Roosevelt Beaufort was hard at work on his memoir. He wore a long winter overcoat and a Russian commissar's fur hat. He'd left his shopping cart, piled with several bulging black plastic bags, out on the empty sidewalk. Franklin was treetop tall and as lean and rugged-looking as a power forward for the Memphis Grizzlies. He must have been a morning regular at the café, because the waitress had greeted him warmly and brought him a steaming cup of that delicious, ardent coffee, which he acknowledged with an abstracted nod.

Franklin looked up at me and frowned. Then he looked back at the pretend keyboard and began to peck again. "The memoir of Franklin Roosevelt Beaufort," he said. "By F. R. Beaufort. I was born to poor but honest sharecroppers in the Mississippi Delta country. Oh, yeah. When I was six, my daddy left home . . ."

Once again, going to work in the cotton fields with his mother was as far as Franklin Roosevelt Beaufort got. He paused, sipped his coffee, resumed work. "The memoir of Franklin . . ."

A couple of construction workers in yellow hard hats came into the café. "Morning, Franklin," one of them said. "How's the memoir coming?"

"Coming just *fine*," Franklin said, quite

fiercely, and leaned in toward his keyboard. "My name is Franklin Roosevelt Beaufort. Yeah. I was born in the Mississippi Delta to honest sharecroppers . . ."

How Charles Dickens would have loved F. R. Beaufort, I thought. How Dickens would have loved the Northeast Kingdom in 1964. How many novels would he have been able to get out of it — a dozen? Two dozen? He'd have shoehorned the Dantean scene of the girlie show at the fair right into *Oliver Twist.*

Prof, for his part, purported to be chagrined and outraged by the live-sex exhibition. He said that since he'd last patronized a girlie revue, as a "young blade," they'd degenerated into something much uglier, and the only reason he'd gone (in disguise) was to apprehend his boys, Big and Little, who had reportedly been seen sneaking under the tent flaps. Still, when it came to initiating me into the rites, wholesome and otherwise, of the Northeast Kingdom, he clearly enjoyed playing Virgil to my Dante.

The following weekend, Prof showed up at Verna's place on Sunday afternoon. "Mosher," he bellowed from the bottom of the stairs leading up to our second-floor rental. "Get your Sunday-school-teaching

ass down here. It's time you met the Leonard boys."

24
THE LEONARD BOYS

The Leonard boys turned out to be three aging brothers who lived in their falling-down family homestead overlooking the falls on the Black River, a few miles north of Orleans. The lane leading up the hill to their place was lined with beat-up pickups and farm trucks. In the backs of some of the trucks were crates containing live roosters. FISH 4 SAIL read a cardboard sign propped against a watering trough fed by a pipe from a spring. Swimming around and around in the trough were a dozen or so huge fall-run brown trout — lunkers — some over twenty inches long. Prof told me that the Leonard boys netted these fish at the falls and sold them, by the pound, to skunked out-of-state fishermen. A second hand-lettered sign, by the caved-in porch steps, read COCKFIGHT TODAY NO WOMEN NO KIDS NO DOGS. It was 1964, and James Dickey had yet to write *Deliverance*. But sitting on the porch, plucking feathers from a heap of dead roosters near an open cellar window, was a boy who could have gotten a walk-on role in the dueling-guitars scene of the movie based on Dickey's novel. Another individual with what appeared to be, and was, a shiny tin nose stood over a makeshift barbecue pit grilling the losers.

"Now, Mosher," Prof said. "This is not your little-kids Sunday school class. Stay close to me and keep your mouth shut and your eyes open."

It was a hot fall afternoon in the Kingdom, but as I followed Prof into the partly collapsed house and down a rickety set of stairs, we were met by a draft of cool, earth-scented air. Milling around on the smooth dirt floor were fifty or sixty men. Along the unmortared granite walls sat stoneware crocks of wine, which, Prof later told me, the Leonards distilled from every berry and wild fruit native to the Kingdom. In the center of the floor was a shallow pit. Around it, in the crepuscular light falling through three small windows, the men formed a tight ring. To see over their heads, we had to stand on the bottom stair. Again Prof cautioned me to stay close to him.

Two men in slouch hats — Teague and Rolly Leonard, Prof whispered to me —

knelt facing each other across the pit. One brother held a tall red rooster, the other the biggest White Leghorn I'd ever seen. Both birds wore three-inch-long razor spurs, shining dully in the dim light. The third brother, Ordney, jostled through the crowd collecting bets. Then, "Fight!" yelled Ordney, and the handlers threw the birds into the pit. As Teague and Rolly jabbed at them, the birds struck out with their spurs. A bloodthirsty roar went up from the bettors as the terrified roosters slashed at each other in a frenzy. Finally, the red bird leaped straight up in the air and came down, spurs first, on the neck of the white. A fine spray of scarlet blood jetted out onto the mob. The battle was over.

Rolly picked up the Leghorn and flung its limp remains out the window onto the growing pile of the vanquished in the dooryard. "Go fry, goddamn you," he growled.

Keep the kids out of the mill? Maybe Phillis and I should do everything in our power to *get the kids out of the Kingdom.* We were discovering, of course, that *no place,* no matter how idyllic, is without its dark underside. While some flatlanders might refer to the Kingdom as "God's country," I could not romanticize this northern fragment of Appalachia if I intended to write

116

about it. The abusive sex shows at the fair and the barbaric cockfights at the Leonard brothers' were as much a part of the Kingdom's traditions and culture as the colorfully dressed, comical straw harvest figures in old-fashioned overalls and sunhats that began to appear on farmhouse porches in early October.

But what about those vivid, Grandma Moses–style primitive paintings that we'd noticed on the sides of barns and covered bridges on our first day in the Kingdom? Who had created these pastoral Vermont landscapes, these scenes of mountains and rivers and lakes and deer and trout and cows lining up at the pasture bars at milking time? Prof told us they'd been painted some twenty years back by a shadowy figure known as the Dog Cart Man. He would appear in the Kingdom now and then in the summer with half a dozen mongrels harnessed, with bits of leather, rope, and baling twine, to a fire engine–red American Flyer wagon. The wagon, Prof said, contained a bedroll, a few cooking utensils, and several gallons of paint in primary colors. For a couple of dollars, a meal, or a corner of a hayloft to bunk in for the night, the Dog Cart Man would paint any rural scene you pleased on the side of your barn or shed, even your house. My favorite was a leaping trout that adorned the Irasburg General Store. But Prof, who knew everything there was to know about local history and who, drunk, sober, or in between, was always happy to share that lore, told me that some years earlier, an impoverished local widow with twelve kids and a five-cow hill farm had sold her eight-year-old son to the Dog Cart Man for fifteen dollars. That night, Prof claimed, the painter attempted to molest the child, whereupon the boy grabbed a rusty old pistol out of the dog cart and shot him through the heart.

Seeing Franklin Roosevelt Beaufort this morning on Beale Street had reminded me that, well into the 1960s, the Kingdom still had plenty of local "characters." Clarence the bottle picker. Joe Canada, the spruce-gum picker, who roamed the woods with a sickle blade attached to a long pole, slicing fresh pitch off spruce trees to sell for chewing gum. A nameless hermit lived in a hemlock-bark shack in the woods northeast of town, and we'd see the occasional tramp up from the railyard for a handout or a bindlestiff working his way from farm to farm in haying time. There seemed to be an unspoken but well-understood code for dealing with these individualists on the fringe of northern New England society. Up to a point, kids were allowed to tease them. Name-calling might be permissible. Rock throwing or setting your dog on a village character — never.

One evening, out for a walk after supper, Phillis and I wandered into Joe Souliere's commission sales barn, behind the village hotel, during the weekly cattle auction. We climbed up to the top of the small grandstand and sat down to watch the proceedings.

"Yes! Here's a pretty little bull calf, boys," Joe chanted into his hand-held microphone as a young Angus was led into the wooden-sided ring. "This gentleman is out of the Kittredge herd up on Guay Hill, he's a good bull, boys, start you a prize herd. Yes! Who'll begin the bidding at twenty dollars? Twenty, twenty, thirty, twenty — thirty? Thirty-five? Forty, do I have forty? I have forty over there. Yes! Fifty dollars, boys? Fifty? Fifty in gold, boys, for this beautiful little bull?"

A fly landed on my nose. I reached up and swatted it away.

"Sold!" Joe barked into the microphone. "For fifty spondaloons to the schoolteacher from New York State."

Phillis couldn't stop laughing, the farmers and village hangers-on in the grandstand around us laughed, but Joe said, "Any motion of the head or hand's a bid, ain't that right, now, boys?"

The schoolteacher from New York had, it seemed, been taken to school. That's how Phillis and I acquired a Black Angus bull we had no earthly use for. He was the first of what would turn out to be a singular menagerie of critters. We kept the little — later not so little — Angus in Verna's barn out behind the house, where he was eventually joined by an intemperate donkey, two intelligent pigs, several laying hens, an orphaned fawn, a pair of very aggressive Toulouse geese, an injured sparrow hawk, a kit fox, and a tiny fisher cat. Many of these animals were gifts from Phillis's students, who assumed that as a science teacher, she could heal, train, raise, and, in the case of the fawn, fox, and fisher, return to the wild, anything on four feet. And that's what she proceeded to do.

The bull-calf debacle was all in good fun. We raised him through the winter as a kind of oversized pet, and Joe Souliere bought him back from me in the spring for exactly what I'd paid. But a week or two after acquiring it, Phillis and I were back at the commission sales, hands tightly folded in our laps like Quakers, as the entire Kittredge herd was auctioned off in an hour. The elderly couple, who'd been on their farm together for nearly sixty years, sat near us in the grandstand. Once I glanced over and noticed that Mr. Kittredge was weeping silently, his tears falling directly onto his barn boots. Joe worked hard to get the Kittredges good value for their cows, but it was a sad, sad night. We'd been in the Kingdom less than two months and already some of it was disappearing before our eyes.

When we had time that fall, we read aloud to each other, scaring ourselves silly with Bram Stoker's *Dracula,* laughing over the incomparably fatuous Mr. Collins in *Pride and Prejudice.* But who would write the stories we were hearing every day right here in the Kingdom? If no one did, they too, like the little farms and big woods of this last Vermont frontier, would soon be gone forever.

25
THE POET AND
THE DEERSLAYER

Just as I remember every detail of the moment when I met Phillis and, later, when our son and daughter were born, so I remember where I was when I met Jim Hayford. It was the week before school started, and we were at a get-together at a colleague's house in Orleans. I remember the green upholstered armchair Jim was sitting in, the bow window behind the chair, the faces of other teachers standing or sitting nearby, even the mill lights glowing in the twilight out the window in the town below.

Jim was the Northeast Kingdom's unofficial poet laureate. He was also the first "real" writer I'd ever known. We spoke that evening about his favorite novelist, Jane Austen, and the rather unlikely friendship between Mr. Darcy and Mr. Bingley. I remarked, with all the wisdom of my twenty-one years, that I couldn't think of many truly great books about friendship. Jim nodded thoughtfully. There really weren't too many, he said. Then, as though these were exceptions to the rule, he quickly mentioned *Moby-Dick, Huckleberry Finn,* and Boswell's *Life of Samuel Johnson.* Not to mention the memorable friendships in the books of my favorite novelist, Dickens.

Jim's conversation had not the slightest didactic flavor. Rather, it was as if Mr. Darcy and Mr. Bingley and Huck and Jim and Ishmael and Queequeg of that true place not to be found on any map were Jim's *own* long-time friends. As, in fact, they were. More than any other person I would ever meet, Jim Hayford had faith in the power of literature and books to transform our lives.

After school the next day I made a beeline to the village library and read Jim's most recent poetry collection, *The Equivocal Sky,* from cover to cover. Yes, there were echoes of Frost in his work, and of Emily Dickinson, too. The vision, though, was pure James Hayford.

The Trouble with a Son

The trouble with a son,
You never get him done.

There's always some defect
Remaining to correct.

Always another flaw
To disappoint his pa —

Who knows how imperfection
May suffer from rejection.

The poet and critic X. J. Kennedy called
Jim Hayford one of "the finest living metri-
cal poets in English." For nearly thirty years
I was fortunate enough to call him my
friend. Like my uncle Reg, Jim was a kind
of surrogate father to me, the Dr. Johnson
to my Boswell. And if I was a son Jim never
"got done," in his presence my youthful
imperfections never "suffered from rejection."

A Vermont native who lived much of his
adult life in the Kingdom, first as a farmer,
carpenter, and piano teacher, then as the
district music teacher, Jim Hayford had
studied poetry under Frost at Amherst College. At graduation, he was awarded the first
Robert Frost Fellowship, which allowed him
to do nothing but write for an entire year.
Frost's only stipulations were that during
the fellowship period Jim must "stay away
from graduate schools, art colonies, big cit-

ies, and Europe," then "produce a book of poems in twenty years."

Jim Hayford was my first personal link to the world of contemporary literature and ideas beyond the Northeast Kingdom and the upstate New York villages where I'd been raised. He was one of the founding members of the American Progressive Party and a Vermont delegate to the 1948 Philadelphia convention that nominated the former vice president Henry Wallace for president on the Progressive ticket. As a result, Hayford had been branded as a communist and, for some years, banned from teaching.

A characteristically brief Hayford poem called "The Waves" captures Jim's alienation from mainstream American politics and, perhaps, from the free-verse trends in poetry espoused by many of his contemporaries:

The green waves mount, crash coolly,
   turn and run.
Their glints are old and new under the
   sun.
The timeless and the temporary are one.

In the emptiness of their uneasy pause
I hear myself recollecting who I was —
Identity, my papers, my lost cause.

I soon realized that Jim Hayford could have excelled in any of the careers he once considered, from the Episcopal priesthood to college teaching. In the end, he chose to live simply in the Northeast Kingdom and to write elegantly simple poems about his life there. While I didn't entirely understand it at the time, Jim's commitment to his writing, and to the home about which he wrote, was precisely the inspiration and example I'd been looking for.

In the meantime, Prof told me that if I wanted to write about the Kingdom, I should get to know Fred Fauchs, a locally renowned trout fisherman, trapper, and deer hunter. As it turned out, Fred looked me up. A spare man in his sixties, with deep seams in his weathered face, he took me fishing to his second-best Northeast Kingdom hot spot, where we cleaned up on pan-sized brook trout. At twenty-one, the former Bad Boy of Chichester fancied himself an accomplished angler. God knows I should have been, after all the hours I'd spent playing hooky and fishing as a kid. And hadn't I learned how to fish from my father and uncle, two of the best fly casters in the Catskill Mountains? A day on the stream with Fred Fauchs disabused me of the notion that I had any particular expertise with a fly rod. Walking along the brook together, we passed a backwater not much larger than a rain puddle, where a recent cloudburst had stranded a pool of standing water about a foot deep and four feet long. Without breaking stride, Fred flipped his worm into the backwater and yanked out an eight-inch-long trout, which he unhooked and tossed into the nearby stream. "Sometimes a fish gets trapped in a place like that," he remarked. Fred used worms exclusively. Like my dad and uncle, I favored flies. He outfished me three or four trout to one.

Fred also introduced me to deer hunting in the Kingdom. My poaching superintendent and I had done some illegal night scouting a few days before the deer season opened, riding the backwoods lanes and logging roads — I drove while he directed a powerful jacklight plugged into the cigarette lighter. But I was flabbergasted to walk into my senior homeroom one November morning and find it nearly empty. It seemed that every boy in the class, and many of the girls as well, had taken the day off to go to deer camp, an annual Northeast Kingdom ritual that, I would learn, had much more to do with family tradition than with hunting.

Deer season opened on the second Saturday of the month. At dusk the following evening, a ten-point buck hung by its antlers in the big maple in Fred Fauchs's yard. Verna told us Fred always had a good buck hanging there by the second evening of the season. Yet Fred scorned the two proven methods of hunting in the Kingdom, driving deer with a group of other hunters and still-hunting (moving slowly through the woods alone). Nor did he hunt from a stand. Instead, Fred walked down his deer.

"A man in good condition can always do it," he told me as we admired the ten-pointer that Sunday evening. "I picked up this old boy's track in the Brownington Bog yesterday at dawn and drove it up over Bald Mountain. I tracked him back around Willoughby Lake through the state forest. I caught sight of him twice, but he was running in heavy timber both times and I hate to wound an animal and not kill it. By dusk last night he was slowing."

"So you came home and got on his track again first thing this morning?"

Fred ran his hand over the dark coat of the deer, collecting a little snow. He shook his head. "It wasn't all that cold last night and I had a blanket. I cut myself a cedar lean-to and lay down on his track. First light, I was on his trail again. He ran across the ice on the Stillwater, over in what we call the Jungle. By noon I was gaining on him pretty steadily. I was trotting. A man, you know, is capable of greater endurance, much more endurance, than a deer. By mid-afternoon he was lying down to rest every fifteen minutes. At sunset I walked up to him, lying under a little fir tree on Barton Mountain, and shot him from fifteen feet away. By then there was a crust on the snow, so I climbed aboard my deer and rode him down the mountainside like a bobsled."

Fred looked at me. "I turned seventy last month. I hope to have many more good hunts, but you never can tell. This was a good hunt."

"Do you ever feel sorry for the deer?"

"Sorry? No, son. This old ridgerunner was nine or ten years old. He'd traveled a lot of fine country. I imagine he bred dozens of does. I could have shot him last year or the year before or the year before that. He had a good, long run."

We stood silently together, looking at the great ridgerunner hanging by his antlers from Fred's hundred-year-old maple. "How far do you think you walked in the past two days?" I asked.

"About thirty-five miles," Fred said. "But only half of that was uphill. Say. Do you and the missus like venison?"

26
VERSAILLES SOUTH AND THE [B]UDGET IN[N]

In early twenty-first-century America, independent bookstores are as endangered as the forests of the Kingdom where Fred Fauchs hunted fifty years ago. Yet one of the many things I love about them is that they're all different. For example, Mary Gay Shipley's fabled That Bookstore in Blytheville (pronounced Bliville), Arkansas, with its stamped-tin ceiling, boxcar geometry, and crimson neon sign flashing the store's distinctive name like a tavern-window beer ad, still looks like the Prohibition-era speakeasy it once was. Mary Gay told me that during the Great Depression, a customer was shot dead sitting in a shoeshine chair where the reading lectern now stands.

TurnRow Book Company in downtown Greenwood, Mississippi, is modeled on a Parisian bookstore, with an elegant book-lined balcony wrapped around a sun-washed atrium containing an assortment of fiction and nonfiction as carefully selected as any you'll find in these United States. The Mississippi writer and bookseller Jamie Kornegay, who manages TurnRow, told me that the store name refers to the space at the end of a cotton row, where the mechanized picker turns around.

In Oxford that evening, however, though I prowled Faulkner's stomping grounds, I could not seem to locate the Reverend Hightower's village house or the Bundren family's farm or the pillared mansion where Thomas Sutpen, as a small boy, was turned away from the front door. Until, that is, I wandered into the southern literature room at Oxford's renowned Square Books. *That's* where I found Faulkner country — a "true place" if one ever existed. Right between the covers of his great novels.

So I'm seeing things. It's come to that. Apparently some comic genie, recently emancipated from his lamp, had scooped up the palace of Versailles, winged his merry way across the Atlantic, and deposited the whole shooting match in Miami, Florida. These were the accommodations that my kind hosts from the local ladies' literary society had arranged for me? Mercy. This five-star oceanside resort hotel wasn't Harold Who's cup of tea. Still, the literary club had bought a couple of hundred copies of my new book, was paying me handsomely, and was feting me that very evening with a dinner in my honor. Surely it would behoove me, for the next several hours, to be on my best behavior.

But wait. Here at a dead run came not one but two big burly doormen, their long doorman's capes flying, to tell the addle-pated elder behind the steering wheel of the rust-bucket Chevy that they're sorry, sir, but in order to stay at Versailles South one needed a reservation.

"Oh, I have one," I called out the window. "That's Mosher, Howard F. But you know what? I'd like to cancel it." And I will be damned if, having not ten seconds ago resolved to comport myself like a sensible human being, I didn't roll right on around the elegantly curved and landscaped drive and back to downtown Miami to seek lodgings more befitting a scribbling storywriter with a radiated prostate gland and a twenty-year-old Celebrity held together with Bondo and clothesline.

UDGET IN proclaimed the cockeyed sign, missing its first and last letters. I pulled into the motel parking lot, swerving to avoid the

132

mummified remains of a large horned toad.

For $22.85, including tax, I managed to secure a room at the [B]udget In[n]. True, upon learning of my change of venue, the literary society no doubt wondered what sort of madman they'd gotten themselves involved with. "Goodness," one of the horrified literati exclaimed, "that's where the homeless people stay!"

Correct. But the dinner and event and signing went "swimmingly," as the same lady graciously told me, and by 11:00 that evening, having regaled Phillis over the phone with an account of my very abbreviated stay at Versailles South, I was ready for bed.

"What's all that racket in the background?" Phillis said. "What sort of place is that motel, anyway? Are you sure you're safe there?"

"Oh, that's just some kids having a party a few rooms down," I said. "Yes, yes, I'm perfectly safe. What was it Verna used to say? I'm as safe as a toad in the palm of God's hand."

From the Vermont end of the line, silence.

"Don't worry, sweetie," I said. "This is a really good place. They let the homeless stay here."

"Lock your door," Phillis said. "Use the

security lock."

Security lock? The [B]udget In[n] was evidently *so* safe a place that they didn't even *need* security locks. I told Phillis that I loved her, and on that happy connubial note our conversation was punctuated by a nearby *crack,* very much resembling that of a pistol shot. "Christ Almighty, a mouse ran up my nightie!" my wife shouted. "BAR-RICADE YOUR DOOR, HOWARD FRANK!"

About midnight what might once have been called in the Deep South a "jollifica-tion" got under way in the room adjacent to mine. Rock concert–volume music, with a thumping, vibrating bass that set the head-board of my bed quivering. An unholy din of screams and laughter. Car doors slam-ming. Screeching tires.

"When you become very tired, Mr. Mosher — *and you will* — you must rest. Do not drive yourself harder. REST."

What was my ultracompetent, entirely businesslike radiation/ oncology nurse do-ing here in Miami at the [B]udget In[n] at 12:02 in the morning? Over the soothing strains of the nocturne next door, I could hear her voice distinctly. How very kind of her to come all this way to check up on me and remind me to REST.

134

Though it runs against my grain to admit it, as my good nurse had warned me, I really was very tired. My stern maiden great-aunt Jane used to say, with a hard look right at me, "Why lie, boy, when the truth serves as well?" Why indeed? Constitutional optimism and the grand old Mosher tradition of flat-out denial will take one only so far in this vale of tribulation, and the fact is, Harold Who was exhausted. But now a herd of North American bison seemed to be stampeding through the room next door — nothing else could possibly account for the thundering. Also, someone was pounding on our shared wall with a sledge hammer. REST, said the no-nonsense nurse. REST, said my friend Dr. Marshall, who had studied with the student of Madame Curie. REST, enjoined the (rather terrifying) National Cancer Institute booklet on prostate radiation therapy.

Jesus of Jerusalem! Neither my good-natured dad nor my irascible uncle would have put up with this ruckus for a Catskill Mountain minute. Barefoot, clad in pj bottoms and T-shirt, I lurched to my feet, padded outside, stepping over the desiccated remains of the horned toad (I made a mental note to bag it up and take it home to show Phillis), and tapped politely on the partyers' door.

A young man holding a red, white, and blue tall boy appeared in the doorway. He was wearing a brand-new pair of cowboy boots and not one stitch else. Behind him was a seething press of similarly unattired young people, America's hope for tomorrow, dancing wildly to a boom box as big as an old-fashioned steamer trunk.

"And you are?" the guy said.

"Howard. Howard Mosher? From the next room over?"

For some reason, this disclosure struck my neighbor, standing there in his birthday suit and boots, with a full-blown Saturnalia going forward in the room behind him, as the funniest thing he'd ever heard. He doubled over with pealing gales of laughter. I laughed, too, I wasn't sure why. Then I said, "I was wondering. If maybe you could pound on the *other* wall for a while? Instead of mine?"

Whereupon, he handed me his tall boy to hold, shouted, "This one's for old Howie," turned around and, naked as a jaybird in snakeskin boots, executed a neat piece of full-tilt broken-field running across the crowded room, driving his right boot clean through the flimsy partition opposite our shared wall.

"Thank you, sir," I said insanely, handing him back his beer, and returned to my room. Was this what my oncology nurse and whoever wrote the NCI posttreatment tips meant when they said REST? Was I, in fact, as I had blithely assured Phillis, as safe as a toad in the palm of God's hand at the [B]udget In[n]? The merrymakers next door did not look homeless. Unless I missed my guess, they were coked-up young rich kids on orgiastic holiday from up north.

Over the infernal racket I heard the welcome sound of a siren, followed shortly by a knocking at my door. *My* door? The evening had attained the surreal hilarity of a madcap late-night-inn scene from a novel by Fielding or Smollett. Except that the young officer standing outside the door seemed very real indeed. And he was not laughing.

"Are you Mr. Howard?"

I gave him my full name and, for reasons that are not clear to me, my social security number.

"Would you be surprised, Mr. Mosher," the officer said, "if I told you that the party in the next room just knocked down half a wall?"

"No sir," I said.

"Would you be surprised if I told you they said you authorized them to do it?"

137

What was the title of that endearing movie with Joe Pesci and Marisa Tomei? The one where two college kids get thrown in a southern jail and charged with murder? And why did it bother me so much that, under these rather more urgent circumstances, I couldn't summon up the name of the film? Fortunately, the officer just shook his head, told me to leave further "interventions" to the Dade County Sheriff's Department, and said goodnight.

As I lay back down on the [B]udget In[n]'s cigarette-scorched bedspread, like a beached Florida weakfish, it occurred to me that this might very well turn out to be my last book tour, American or otherwise. Surely tonight had to be the nadir of my fellowship period. If I could just get through until dawn without being shot, trampled, hospitalized for exhaustion, or arrested, matters had to improve. Somehow or other, I still had faith that all of this foolishness — my so-called writing career, the book tour, my attempt to stave off, through radiation, what is probably nature's way of keeping us from turning into vegetables — would all work out for the best.

Wouldn't it?

■ ■■ ■

PART II
HOPE

■ ■■ ■

27
TAKING STOCK IN LUCINDA WILLIAMS COUNTRY

As in the silly old conundrum about the chicken and the egg, I've never been able to decide which comes first, faith or hope. A cynic might say that faith is what we fall back on when we run out of hope. A strict evolutionist might add that faith, at least when it comes to an afterlife, is a psychological extension of our survival instinct. To me, faith boils down to the belief that, as Uncle Reg liked to remind me, "It's a glorious thing just to live." That may not be a lot to go on, metaphysically speaking. But when it comes to faith in the basic goodness of life, it seems like a promising starting point.

Hope, on the other hand, strikes me as a more modest sentiment. For me, hope has little to do with metaphysics and a lot to do with the here and now. It is the day-to-day credo of farmers, teachers, doctors, writers, and baseball players who, even when they're on a tear, are probably going to make at

least two outs for every clean base hit —
but look forward to each upcoming at-bat
with optimism and excitement.

On the evening after my interlude in the
[B]udget In[n], I took inventory over the
phone with Phillis from my motel in Beau-
mont, Texas. The practical purpose of an
author's tour, of course, is to sell the
author's latest book. How many of mine had
I sold thus far? Well, several thousand more
than I would have had I used my fellowship
period to stay at home in Vermont and
REST. I'd met dozens of marvelously independent and knowledgeable booksellers,
augmented my personal library with thirty
or so great new (and old) titles, weathered
an attack review, and had a chance to tell
my audiences about the roller-coaster ride
of our first year in Vermont, when it often
seemed that we were living on hope and
hope alone.

Certainly that was the case when it came
to my hope to write the stories of the
Kingdom.

Phillis and I were busier than we'd ever
been in our lives. Besides teaching, we attended covered-dish suppers, put on pag-
eants with the Sunday school, and drove
over the Green Mountains to Burlington

many nights and weekends to take graduate courses. I showed my new friend and colleague Jim Hayford a draft of my master's-thesis proposal on Shakespeare's villains. "This is all well and fine," Jim told me. "Just don't neglect your *own* stories."

Sometimes in the evening we'd slip away from grading stacks of papers, cut across the footbridge over the river by the mill we'd been enjoined to *keep the kids out of,* and climb the hill to 5 Cliff Street for a cup of tea and a restorative visit with the Hayfords. Those evenings remain some of the best of our lives. We'd talk about everything under the sun, coax Jim and Helen into telling us Northeast Kingdom ghost stories, and listen to Jim read aloud from *The Life of Samuel Johnson.*

As a child, Jim had been quite frail. In the thirty years I knew him, I was never able to talk him into going trout fishing with me. He was the best speaker I'd ever heard, but he shied away from large groups. Otherwise the most skeptical of Northeast Kingdom Vermonters, Jim was utterly persuaded that the plays of Shakespeare, which he knew and loved as much as if he'd written them himself, had been composed not by the glover's son from Stratford-on-Avon but by Edward de Vere, the seventeenth Earl of

Oxford. I took the more conventional side, and we amiably debated the question for the rest of Jim's life.

Best of all, Jim and Helen Hayford, who were keenly interested in local history, introduced us to the stories of the Northeast Kingdom in ways no one else could. One evening they took us on a picnic to the Brownington Stone House, a four-story former boarding school a few miles north of Orleans. The Stone House was built in 1835 by the Reverend Alexander Twilight, whom Middlebury College claims as the first African American college graduate. Perched on a hilltop overlooking much of the northern Kingdom, it is a great mystery. To this day no one knows exactly where its beautifully cut granite blocks came from or how Twilight, working with a team of oxen, constructed the building. We loved sitting with the Hayfords atop Prospect Hill, overlooking the Kingdom from the Willoughby Gap in the east to Jay Peak in the west, to Lake Memphremagog, stretching north deep into the mountains of Canada, and to the Cold Hollow Mountains in the south. Jim pointed out Allen Hill, a few miles to the west, granted to General Ira Allen, Ethan's brother, for his service in the Revolutionary War. And Lake Willoughby, the setting of Robert Frost's terrifying poem of madness and isolation, "A Servant to Servants."

From Prospect Hill the Hayfords traced out for us the route followed by the Bayley-Hazen Military Road, built during the Revolutionary War by a crew of bold Vermont hearties with the modest intention of invading and annexing Canada. And just west of Jay Peak, in 1856, a band of Irish Fenians mounted their own grand invasion of Quebec. (They were promptly driven back over the border by a few angry local farmers armed with muskets and pitchforks.) Some miles to the north, in the flat farming country of the St. Lawrence River Valley, Dr. William Henry Drummond had written his popular French Canadian dialect poems "The Habitant" and "The Voyageur," and as dusk settled over the mountains, Jim recited passages from them. History and literature had never seemed this immediate to me before. How could it be that no one had written fiction about this wondrous kingdom without a king?

As if he'd read my thoughts, Jim, with his kind eyes and long, ascetic scholar's face, said to me, "About ten years ago I worked up the courage to read one of my poems aloud to Robert Frost. We were sitting on the front porch of his cottage at Breadloaf. 'Well, Hayford,' he said when I finished, 'I wouldn't say that the way you do. But I have to remember that you need to go at things your way. You've found your way. You've found your own voice.' "

Jim looked off at the miles of mountains, purple in the fall dusk. With a flicker of a smile he said, "It had taken me nineteen years to find that voice. I guess waiting for it is what hope is all about. Maybe you'll find yours quicker. It all comes down to application, you know. Application of the seat of the pants to the seat of the chair."

I hoped so. But now, as I talked with Phillis from my rundown motel on the Louisiana-Texas state line where I had just discovered five black-as-night, deadly poisonous toadstools as big around as dessert saucers growing beside the empty in-room bar (shades of the [B]udget In[n]!), what I really hoped was that those two 24-karat-gold staples that Dr. Marshall had fired into my ailing prostate to help minimize damage to the adjacent plumbing critical to one's, ah, romantic capabilities, had done the trick.

Pray Jesus, no, I thought, trying not to look at those toadstools, an image that I feared might have the same long-term effect. I was sorely tempted to jump into the Loser Cruiser and head straight home to the love of my life in Vermont.

"I'm sure your romantic capabilities will be fine, hon," Phillis reassured me. "And think of the stories you'll have to tell me from the rest of your tour."

True. Still, as we said goodbye, Phillis from Kingdom County and I from the Toadstool Motel two thousand miles away, I could not have envisaged all that lay ahead of me in the next month or who I would meet along the way.

28
Two Lone Star Hitchhikers

At Houston's "premier literary market-place," as the *New York Times* has called Brazos Bookstore, I bought a copy of Oliver Sacks's latest book. The following morning, at a McDonald's on the eastern fringe of San Antonio, I read a chapter. Sacks, who wrote one of my all-time favorite books, *The Man Who Mistook His Wife for a Hat,* probably knows more about certain kinds of savantism than any other man or woman alive. He searches out the most idiosyncratic geniuses of our times, real-life counterparts of the Don Quixotes of literature, and, with respect and affection, he celebrates their individualism, their nearly superhuman abilities, and their dignity. He is also a wonderful writer and, by crikey, there in the parking lot of Mickey D's, thumbing a ride up to the Alamo, was the great man himself.

"So, Dr. Sacks," I said, pulling back onto I-10 and coaxing the Loser Cruiser up to its maximum nonshimmying speed of 58.5 mph. "I've wanted to meet you for a long time."

"Thank you, Mr. Mosher. And I you."

Oh?

Hurrying on, "I mean, Doctor, I love, absolutely *love,* your stuff. Great reads . . . transformative experience . . . funny . . ." Fiddlesticks. I didn't have the faintest notion what to say to an author I admired.

The gracious Dr. Sacks seemed genuinely pleased. "Why, that's very kind of you to say so."

"I wonder if you might be willing to . . ." Extending my copy of his new book toward him. "I don't know where you usually like to sign your —"

"Of course," he said, opening the book to the title page and inscribing, very neatly, under his printed name, "To my fellow author, Howard Mosher, with great interest, Oliver Sacks."

With great interest? Good Jesus. Dr. Sacks had not appeared out of nowhere just to bum a ride over to the Alamo. No. He had traveled — traveled a very great distance — to *examine* me.

What a kindly gentleman was the learned Oliver. I felt I could tell the famous alienist anything.

"Ever since I was a small boy, Dr. Sacks, I've imagined myself carrying on conversations with Huckleberry Finn and Tom Sawyer, not to mention Roderick Usher from 'The Fall of the House of Usher' and sometimes David Copperfield . . ."

Out popped Dr. Sacks's notepad. "This is most intriguing. You actually *hear* their voices talking to you?"

"Yes, yes! Dead authors, in my head. Lots of them. Sometimes they all natter away at the same time."

What had come over me? That business about the voices jabbering all at once, like a scene from *The Exorcist,* was a boldfaced lie.

"Is hearing voices bad?" I inquired, with the sly sidelong smile of the perfectly mad.

"Not necessarily," the doctor said. He was writing rapidly now. "Not as long as the voices don't tell you to do bad things."

And suddenly, despite my long training as a prevaricating novelist, the truth spilled out. "I'm afraid," I said, "that they told me to be a writer."

The doctor's pen paused mid-word: "Patient reports full-blown audio hallucin—" His face looked very, very grave.

"Not," Dr. Sacks said, "a *writer?*"

I nodded.

Oliver flipped his notepad shut and tucked it into the breast pocket of his white coat. "In that case, Mr. Mosher," he said quietly, "I'm afraid that there's nothing I can do for you."

There's no better place to begin a tour of an American city than the regional history and literature section of its independent bookstore. At San Antonio's fine independent, The Twig, which bears an uncanny resemblance to a modern-day Alamo, I discovered a whole shelf devoted exclusively to the works of the Texas author John Graves. I snapped up a copy of *Goodbye to a River,* Graves's account of a 1950s canoe trip down a stretch of the upper Brazos that was about to be dammed. An hour later, ambling along San Antonio's downtown river walk, I wondered how many of the hundreds of tourists who take this stroll each day know anything about the history of Graves's beautiful river and the Conquistadors who ventured up it in their "dented armor" but "didn't stick."

WATCH YOUR STEP. NATIVE TEXAS LANDSCAPE. The discreet sign peeking out of the sky-blue bluebells at the rest area between San Antonio and Austin gave me pause. It

was as pithy as Gus McCrae's WE DON'T
RENT PIGS sign in *Lonesome Dove.* But
what did it mean? Was it an injunction,
Lone Star–style, not to step on the wildflowers? Or a heads-up to watch out for a stray
sidewinder? Whichever, I liked the sign a
lot. I whipped out my notebook, and when
I looked up again, there he was. One beat-up
cowboy boot cocked against the WATCH
YOUR STEP sign. His once-white cowboy
hat raked back on his brow. A face the color
and texture of a hundred-year-old Mexican
saddle. Looking right straight at me. A
Corona in one hand, in the other a cardboard sign: HOPE SPRINGS ETERNAL. AMA-
RILLO OR BUST.

Big as life. Right out of the blue southwestern sky and Harold Who's perfervid
imagination. The West Texas Jesus.

29
WINTER IN THE KINGDOM

"Tell me about those Vermont winters," the West Texas Jesus was saying, opening another Corona and settling into the catbird seat like a man easing onto a stool at his favorite neighborhood bar. "Are they really as long and cold as I've heard?"

"Longer and colder," I said in the grim tone Vermonters reserve for discussions concerning inclement weather and obituaries in the local weekly. And with that I was off and running on our first winter in the Kingdom.

Once the leaves have fallen in northern New England, I told my new traveling partner, you can see the true lay of the land, the bones of the country, and, if you search for it, an astonishing array of wildlife. Over our Thanksgiving break, while skiing up Irasburg Mountain, Phillis and I came across a perfect imprint of a great horned owl. The bird had evidently dived into the snow, talons first, wings outspread, after a mouse or vole. Every feather was as distinct as a photographic negative, and the wing-span was wider than my outstretched arms. Later that day we discovered the remains of a barred owl and a goshawk, their talons gripped in mortal combat. Neither bird had been willing to release its hold on the other, so they had plunged to the ground and died like two battling deer locked by their antlers. Near a frozen beaver pond we watched, helpless, as a mink and a muskrat fought to the death. The mink had a death hold on the muskrat's neck, but the rat had chewed one of its adversary's hind feet almost completely off. When I tried to separate the combatants with my ski pole, they tumbled onto the ice on the pond and broke through. Even in the frigid water, they continued to fight.

One day at school the following week, my seniors became involved in a discussion over which wild animal was the fiercest. Polar bear, Becca said. Another student had read that, ounce for ounce, the fiercest animal on earth was the tiny shrew. They were interested to learn that the Romans, putting the question to the test in the Colosseum, had discovered that with a single swipe, a European brown bear could break the neck of the largest lion. Bill the brain pointed out that man himself was no slouch when it came to sheer savagery, citing not only Genghis Khan and Attila the Hun but a recent account he'd read of the Battle of Gettysburg. Yet the fiercest, most fearless wild animal I have ever seen was a bird that Phillis and I encountered in the winter woods of the Kingdom.

The early winter of 1964–65 was, we were told, an especially rough one throughout Vermont, with even deeper cold and more snow than usual. It was also one of those winters when the snowshoe-hare population in the far Canadian north had reached a low point, driving boreal hawks and owls south for food. Early in December, in a small birch tree overlooking a field on the edge of Orleans, we spotted a great gray owl, ordinarily a denizen of the Canadian taiga, surveying the countryside with his huge, spectacled eyes. Next, snowy owls began to appear. One took up a vigil atop the TV antenna of the downtown theater in Newport, making an occasional foray out over Lake Memphremagog to scavenge the discarded heads of perch and smelt scattered around ice-fishing shanties. Sadly, some Kingdom outlaw shot it. Just over the border in Canada was a commercial pheasant farm. When a snowy began snatching pheasants for dinner, the owner stretched a tough netting material across the top of the pen. The white owl crashed into the net, which sagged down onto the pheasants, then it yanked one of the captive birds through the hole it had ripped and soared off with its prey.

One twilight when Phillis and I were skiing along a logging trail, we came upon a great snowy devouring a freshly killed hare just ahead in the path. Mantling over the bloody rabbit, the owl arched its wings, as if defying us to take another step, and stared at us with its great yellow eyes. After a minute it flew into a nearby spruce tree, and we circled out around it. A few yards down the trail, we looked back. The bird had returned to its meal and was busy pulling out the rabbit's innards. Hurrah for great snowy owls! Hurrah for the Northeast Kingdom!

It was dark when we came out of the woods and looked down on the lights of the village that was becoming our home. How could we ever leave a place so rich in friends, wilderness and wildlife, history and stories? Like the sleigh driver in the Frost poem, I had promises to keep, to myself and to Phillis, to move on and become a writer.

But I was feeling torn between those hopes and my growing attachment to the Kingdom, where I was beginning to find my material, if not yet my voice. Skiing back down the mountain, I vowed to myself to make a renewed effort to finish writing our landlady's moonshining story and a deer-poaching tale I'd started recently. If I could muster just a fraction of the determination and single-mindedness of the Arctic owl we'd encountered, I could write those stories.

The night before, poring over Jim Hayford's copy of *The Life of Samuel Johnson,* I'd come across Johnson's oft-cited remark to Boswell on their great journey to the Hebrides: "A man may write at any time if he will set himself doggedly to it." Hadn't Jim — my personal Dr. Johnson — said that it all came down to application of the seat of the pants to the seat of the chair?

I went home and doggedly applied the seat of my pants to the seat of the chair and wrote straight through the night, finishing both stories. They were a start. Dr. Johnson had also said that the art of writing was "attained by slow degrees." Except, perhaps, for the Battle-ax's remark to us, there was no blueprint waiting out there, in graduate school or anywhere else. And there sure as hell weren't any shortcuts. I realized that I was flying on hope alone.

30

On the Austin City Limits with the West Texas Jesus

He was propped up against the rickety headboard of the other bed in our Motel 6 room on the outskirts of Austin, still wearing his boots and hat, a Corona wedged between the torn-out knees of his jeans, telling me his story, which sounded like some footloose loser's in a Kris Kristofferson song.

The West Texas Jesus (Spanish pronunciation *hay-zeus*) was an out-of-work carpenter. Weekends he played pedal steel and sang backup in a five-piece Texas band. You know, the kind that performs in roadhouses behind chicken wire strung up to protect them from flying beer bottles? Though he didn't come right out and say so, I strongly suspected he'd been kicked out of the group for chronic drunkenness. Like his namesake, my Jesus was full of stories and advice, solicited and otherwise. As for his singing, well, the old *caballero* tried to sound like

Kristofferson. But where Kris's voice was gravelly, this guy's was simply shot from tens of thousands of unfiltered Luckies and more six-packs than a body could count.

Here we were, then, on a Sunday evening in a cheap motor court in Austin, home of *Austin City Limits* as well as a lively literary community centered around BookPeople Bookstore, including the three book people who'd made up the entire audience at my reading there earlier in the evening. That's right. My Austin fan base consisted of the store's events coordinator, her assistant, who was "in and out" (mostly out), and my former next-door neighbor from back in the Kingdom, who'd recently moved to Texas. Plainly, the farther I ventured from New England, the tougher it was going to be to generate good audiences.

"Look, Mosher, speaking of hope," the West Texas Jesus said, slinging a red-bound Gideon Bible over onto the standard Motel 6 purple coverlet on my bed — which coverlets, I'd heard, got washed every six months whether they needed it or not. "You're hoping for answers to this touring gig, right? Flip open that Bible to any old page and read a verse. You won't believe how helpful it'll be. I do it all the time."

I opened the Bible, at random, to Numbers 15: "While the children of Israel were in the wilderness, they found a man who gathered sticks upon the Sabbath day . . . and the Lord said to Moses, the man shall be surely put to death; all the congregation shall stone him with stones without the camp."

"Good God!" I shouted, hurling the Gideon back at the beer-drinking Jesus. "What are you trying to tell me? That I should be stoned for doing an event on a Sunday?"

He held up his hands. "Hell, no," he said. "If you'll remember, I changed all that when I was out gleaning somebody else's wheat one Sunday with those twelve slackers. Look here now. Try her again. Use a different book this time."

From my stack on the bedside table he selected Elaine Pagels's interpretation of *The Secret Gospel of Thomas,* which I'd bought earlier that evening at BookPeople, mainly so that the store would be able to record at least one sale at the end of my event. He opened it to a Books-a-Million bookmark — how did *that* get in there? — and cited Thomas citing him. "He who brings forth that which is within himself will be saved by that which he brings forth. He who does not bring forth that which is within himself will be destroyed by that which he does not bring forth."

If this admonition was meant for me, it seemed nearly as ominous as the threat from Numbers to stone me to death for reading to three people on a Sunday. What, precisely, was I supposed to "bring forth"?

I started to ask the West Texas Jesus what he'd do in my place, but he just grinned and said *he'd* begin by asking the right question.

"Which is?"

"What *you're* going to do in your place," he said. "In the meantime, tell me a little story. You're a storyteller, aren't you? Tell me about that other time when you asked for my help. Up on that ski lift."

"How do you know about that?" I said. The West Texas Jesus tapped his head in a canny way, cracked open another Corona, and settled back.

31
WHY I AM A CROSS-COUNTRY SKIER, PART 1

The conditions that morning were ideal for skiing. The temperature was about ten degrees above zero. It was clear and windless. Several inches of new snow covered the dooryard, glowing with a lovely bluish tint in the dawn light. Having finally finished a draft of our landlady's story and another story besides, I thought I'd celebrate by taking a day to go skiing. I slid my skis into our beat-up station wagon and drove to a resort a couple of hours away. I bought my lift ticket, then waited a few minutes for the chairlift to start operating. I was the first and, so far, the only customer.

I'd chosen a medium-length trail, somewhere between half and three-quarters of a mile long, and it appeared that I'd have it entirely to myself, at least for the first run down. Though noticeably colder here on the mountain, it was a splendid morning. As I rose, effortlessly, up the slope, I counted more than twenty other peaks, their snowy tops glowing as pink as strawberry ice cream in the sunrise. Already I was anticipating the matchless exhilaration of a clean, swooping downhill run on brand-new powdery snow.

Floating up the mountain fifteen to twenty feet over the tops of snow-laden evergreens, I shivered slightly. Like many local skiers, I scorned fashionable ski wear, and instead was dressed in long johns, wool pants, a couple of flannel shirts under a sweater, a red-and-black-checked hunting jacket, and a red wool hunting cap with earflaps. A breeze had come up, and the air sparkled with crystalline flakes of ice, like hoar frost. Each time the chair rolled under a lift tower, it made a small thud, like a kiddie ride at a fair. Riding a chairlift is like going up in a safe and stable Ferris wheel at an innocent country carnival.

The lift line inclined at a steeper slant. My chair stopped. All the chairs on the lift stopped. It was totally silent. Alone in midair, I was out of sight of the ski lodge below and the landing deck on the mountaintop above.

Of course, this had happened to me before. All ski lifts stop occasionally, usually for reasons obscure to their riders. Soon enough the chairs would start to move again, and I'd be on my way. They didn't, though, and I wasn't. I sat waiting in that big wooden-and-steel contraption, swaying in the gathering breeze, and nothing happened at all. What was I supposed to do? Call for help on my cell phone? This was 1964. My feet were getting cold. So were my mittened hands. I stamped one foot, then the other, on the metal ski rest, rattling my wooden skis like deer antlers. There was no response, just the enveloping, now vaguely unsettling, silence. I noticed that it had begun to snow. The breeze had picked up into a gusting wind.

Higher up the slope, a grooming machine on caterpillar treads emerged from the thickening snowflakes. I waved my hunting cap at the driver, who looked warm and content inside his glass-enclosed cab. He took a sip from a large blue thermos as I signaled frantically. He glanced up at me, smiled, and waved back. Then he swung off onto a parallel trail for advanced skiers and started back up the mountainside.

In no particular order, I began to catalog the things I had not done in my twenty-one short years. Fish the rivers of Labrador. Have kids with Phillis. Publish a story. God in heaven, right now I'd settle for getting my stiffening feet back on terra firma again.

I swore, *swore,* that if the powers that be would let me live to revise Verna's moon-shining story (yes, and publish it), I would never again waste a precious morning in such a frivolous way. What the hell was the matter with me? This wasn't a life-or-death situation. Was it? It was getting colder by the minute. And exactly who was I beseeching to come to my rescue? In the King James Bible, God is recorded as laughing just once. I could see the old boy we'd been teaching our Sunday school kids about, with His fiery punishments and stern injunctions, laughing again this morning. Laughing at me, stuck up here *freezing to death on a goddamn chairlift.*

A desperate strategy occurred to me. It was hard to estimate, but I guessed I was suspended thirty-five to forty feet above the ground. Itinerant roofers I'd worked with in college — a hard-bitten outfit, if I do say so — had a grim adage. With luck, they liked to say, a man might survive a twenty-or even a twenty-five-foot fall. Thirty feet was considered the cutoff point, the gateway to that bourne from which few men, even hard-bitten roofers, return. But if I unclasped my bindings, kicked out of my skis, and hung from the footrest by my hands, I could perhaps get into that thirty- to thirty-five-foot range where survival was still an outside possibility. There were, after all, less yielding surfaces than snow to fall on.

It was storming harder. The narrow corridor of trail through the woods below was filling up with new snow. Whose woods they were I knew very well — they belonged to the Christly corporation that owned the resort and the mountain, whose lift operators were even now drinking coffee, gabbing, checking the scores of last night's high school basketball games in the morning paper. That was it! No other skiers had shown up yet, so in the absence of customers, *they had shut off the lift and forgotten all about me.* Enough. I'd give the doughnut-eating bastards five minutes, not a second more. Then, while I still had some faint sensation left in my hands, I'd make the plunge. Maybe I was only thirty feet off the ground, which did seem closer in the snow squall, didn't it? No, it did not. Was this pickle I was in a metaphor for my first year as a teacher? Or for the apprenticeship of an aspiring novelist? I didn't know or care. I just wanted to get off that chairlift, and off that mountain, alive.

"Wouldn't you?" I said to the West Texas Jesus, on the outskirts of Austin, forty-some years later.

Nothing. I repeated the question. No response. What a comedown. The guy had fallen asleep right in the middle of my story, leaving me hanging up there in the wind and snow, at the mercy of the elements and our heavenly father.

32
WHY I AM A CROSS-COUNTRY SKIER, PART 2

With an anticlimactic jerk, as I was telling the West Texas Jesus the next morning somewhere between Tucumcari and Albuquerque, the chairlift started again. Up the mountain I went, too numb to feel anything more than relief. Ahead, on a jagged outcropping of granite above the treeline, perched the operator's booth. Uncertain whether I could even stand up, I motioned for the attendant to slow down the lift. Maybe I could warm up in his booth, then catch a ride down to the lodge in the groomer. I called out for the guy to stop the chairs. He was bent over a paperback book and didn't seem to hear me. At the far end of the landing, the empty chairs were whipping around an elevated bull wheel before starting back down the mountainside. Perhaps I could just stay aboard, ride back to the lodge, have a cup of coffee, and reconnoiter. But to judge from the way the

169

chairs were snapping past that wheel, at the very least I'd get whiplash and be out of commission for weeks. "Whiplash?" said the counsel for the ski resort, all but winking at the jury of frowning Vermont working men and working women, all twelve of whom would know better than to get on a chairlift in the first place. This was how young teachers and would-be writers spent their time? Paying cash money to ride uphill in order to slide back down again? Damages of $0 awarded. Court costs assigned to the plaintiff.

Touchdown was now scant seconds away. I flipped up the bar, stood, and let the seat shove me along over the snowy landing by the backs of my half-frozen legs — which promptly gave way beneath me. Down I went, ass over teakettle. Luckily, the chair passed harmlessly above me, but before I could crawdad my way to safety, the next one whanged hard, really hard, into my back and shoulders. Still wearing my skis, I rolled straight into the path of the next chair. I tried to fend it off with my left ski pole, which snapped neatly in two. What if one of those eighty-pound conveyances whapped me a good one in the head? How many novels would I write then? And why didn't the kid in the booth shut down the lift? They hadn't hesitated to stop it when I was dangling thirty-five feet up in the air in a whiteout.

"Turn it off!" I bellowed.

The operator looked up from his book. Instead of shutting off the lift, he rushed out of the booth and screamed, "What are you doing, you dumb son of a bitch?"

His response was of a piece with everything else that had happened to me in the last twenty minutes. After all, I wasn't supposed to be flopping around on the mountaintop dodging chairs. I was supposed to be dead, frozen stiff as a human icicle, from my little airing-out high above the mountainside. The next chair cracked into my right ski as I tried again to flip out of the way. I felt like a snapping turtle on its back in the middle of a busy freeway. What if my collar or belt got caught on a bar and drew me into the bull wheel to be pulled limb from limb like a victim of the Inquisition? Would that satisfy them?

"Turn it off!" I brayed.

The operator stood glaring down at me. I had assumed a semifetal position with my arms protecting my head. "Why didn't you say you didn't know how to dismount properly?" he shouted.

Apparently we were to debate the issue

while I was being mauled to death by chairs. At that point, my survival instincts kicked in.

"I'll get you!" I yelled insanely, lashing out at him with the stump of my broken ski pole.

Miraculously, I managed to scuttle out of the way of the chairs. I staggered to my feet and made a last, ineffectual lunge at the operator with my good pole as he fled into his booth. Where, at last, he saw fit to press the shut-off button.

Not one thing that had happened after the lift stopped, stranding me halfway up the mountain, made a particle of sense to me. What I did next, however, did. Without further ado, I hobbled over to one of the trails, shoved off with my unbroken pole, and started down the mountainside.

The trackless new snow was as light and fine as confectioner's sugar. The lift overhead was running smoothly. A middle-aged couple riding up the mountain in identical red parkas waved, a ski bum dressed in jeans and a sweatshirt gave me a thumbs-up. In the freshly groomed snow, I turned sharply in little upflung flurries, sped grandly around sweeping curves, traversed long, steep pitches as if I were a truly expert skier. Even with just one functional pole, it was the most glorious downhill run of my life. And the last.

At the bottom of the hill I executed a neat turn-stop. I unbuckled my bindings, shouldered my battered skis, and made straight for the ski shop in the basement of the lodge. "I'd like to trade these in on a new pair of cross-country skis," I told the guy at the counter. "Don't ask me why."

33
THE GREAT SOUTHWEST

The American Southwest is a geography of bright colors. Red sandstone outcroppings. Irrigated green fields of alfalfa. The desert in blossom. And wide, blue rivers.

I could not seem to stay away from rivers. Here I was at five in the afternoon in Albuquerque, moseying along on foot through the big cottonwoods lining the fabled Rio Grande, for the love of Pete. The breeze off the water sifted through the rustling gray-green cottonwood leaves overhead — fleetingly, I imagined they were saying "Keep the kids out of the mill." I thought of Rangers McCrae and Call of *Lonesome Dove* crossing this river on the eve of their great American odyssey to steal back their horses from the old Mexican bandit Pedro Flores, and I thought of the borderlands ballads of Marty Robbins, and I will be damned if it didn't occur to me, right out of the cobalt New Mexican sky, that I was taking this trip in part *to see if I could.* A little 20,000-mile, 100-city, 190-store confidence course *to prove to myself that I could still see the U. S. of A. on less than one hundred dollars a day in a 1980s Chevy beater with 291,000 — no, make that 294,480 miles — on the odometer.*

"Listen," I said to the West Texas Jesus as we walked along the riverbank together, killing time before my evening event at Albuquerque's excellent independent, Bookworks. "Can I tell you something?"

"I don't know," he said, flinging his just-drained empty into the river and opening a fresh one. "Can you?"

"I want to tell you a story," I persisted. "About some unfinished business with my deceased uncle."

"If this involves money, I don't want to hear it," the Jesus said. "You know I'm not interested in money. Never have been."

"What about your yarn of the good and faithful servant who increased his master's talents? That involves money."

"What about it? The money wasn't the point. The point, Mr. Writer Man, is how are *you* going to use your talents over the next while. 'Bring forth that which is within,' so to speak. In the meantime, I know all about your unfinished business with your uncle. That's between you two to work out."

"Do you know about the legacy?" I said. "Since you seem to know so damn much?"

"As a matter of fact, I do," he said. "And I know that you need to put all that behind you. You need to think about what you want *your* legacy to be. You're the writer here."

He reached into his hip pocket and magically produced another ice-cold Corona. "Here," he said. "Drink this, Harold, and lighten up."

The place sat alone in the desert, a concrete-block, bunkerlike affair with a single rusted gas pump and not another building in sight in any direction. I was somewhere between Albuquerque and Phoenix, and the air was as hot as the smelting room of a steel mill. An outdoor thermometer in the shape of an old-fashioned Coca-Cola bottle hung at a cockeyed slant beside the store's screen door: 112 degrees.

As I pumped my gas, a woman pushing a shopping cart resolved out of the heat waves. She was dark-complected, with long black hair. She might have been thirty, she might have been fifty. I couldn't guess because, in the shimmering heat rays, she looked absolutely apparitional.

She began sorting through the trash bar-

176

rel beside the pump, came up empty, and went into the store a minute ahead of me. I arrived at the counter just in time to witness the following transaction. The shopping-cart woman was holding a pint of milk, which the clerk had just rung up. On the far end of the counter sat a small black-and-white television set tuned to the Arizona Diamondbacks' game.

"You're eight cents short," the clerk said, pointing at the coins on the counter.

And right then, I made my worst mistake of the trip. Waiting for the clerk to say *No problem* or *Close enough* or *Catch you next time* and hand over the bottle of milk to the woman, I hesitated. Distracted by my own petty thoughts and by the baseball game on the snowy TV, I failed to act. Not for long. Maybe a second or two. But that was all it took.

By the time I reached for my wallet and, like Martina McBride in her song "Love's the Only House," said "I'll cover that," the shopping-cart woman was out the door. The pint of milk sat on the counter, stark as a guilty verdict.

"Wetback," the clerk said. "She came in here with three kids last night at rush hour wanting to redeem bottles they'd picked up along the road."

Not waiting for my change, I rushed outside with the milk, into the blasting heat. The parking lot was empty. How could this be? Not fifteen seconds had passed since the woman had left the store. I could see for hundreds of feet in every direction. There was no place to hide, and no vehicle had stopped or even passed by since I'd pulled up to the pump. But she'd vanished, along with her cart, as mysteriously as she'd appeared. My opportunity to be of some help to somebody other than my sorry self had vanished with her.

The former president of the American Booksellers Association, bookseller nonpareil Gayle Shanks, had drummed up a great audience for me that evening at Changing Hands Bookstore in Tempe, on the south edge of Phoenix. Gayle told me that when the store was struggling through its early years and on the brink of failure, a network of local women, all avid readers, had formed several book groups expressly designed to keep the store afloat. *They* certainly hadn't failed to act and let an opportunity to help their community slip away.

When I settled into my sleazy motel on the outskirts of Phoenix that night, I was still angry with myself. My father *never* would have hesitated, back in that convenience store in the desert, before reaching for his thin schoolteacher's wallet. My storytelling uncle Reg would have made the good Samaritan himself look mingy-spirited. Phillis would have taken the woman and her kids home and befriended them.

"*You'd* have helped that Mexican lady," I said to the West Texas Jesus. "The one with the shopping cart. Wetback or no."

"I hope so, señor," he said with a slight south-of-the-border accent I hadn't really noticed before. "How do you think *I* got here?"

34
SWEEPING UP IN EL DORADO

It is widely held that as members of our dubious species grow older, they require less sleep. I have never been much of a sleeper. I've always been afraid I'd miss something important I might want to write about. What might I be missing at 4:30 a.m. on a foggy summer morn in the vicinity of my Motel 6 in Oakland? I had no idea. But as usual, I was already up and doing, with all of the unswerving, slightly crazed purposefulness of a small-town busybody.

So in the early light of this Bay Area dawn, nothing would suffice but that I jog the mile or so along the water to Jack London Square and its famous open market to see what I could see. En route I reflected on what I had accomplished in sunny California over the past week. I'd visited a couple dozen of the best independent bookstores in the country, including Vroman's in Pasadena and Village Books in Pacific

Palisades. And yes, I'd walked the swelter-
ing streets of downtown LA with Uncle
Reg, in the footsteps of Raymond
Chandler's detective hero, Philip Marlowe.
And I had prowled the hills and waterfront
of San Francisco with an eye out for that
short, fat human Gatling gun of a private
eye, Dashiell Hammett's Continental Op.
Finding him at last right where I had found
Faulkner's people back in Mississippi — in
the city's great independent bookstores.
And, oh my, how proud my uncle would
have been — how proud, and humbled *I* was
— to discover a few of my own novels not
far from Chandler's and Hammett's in City
Lights' great fiction section, just a few short
steps away from the famous sign, hand-
lettered by the store's poet-owner, Lawrence
Ferlinghetti: NO SHIRT NO SHOES FULL
SERVICE. It brought tears to my eyes. (Or
was it the signed but still unsold copy of my
novel *A Stranger in the Kingdom,* which I had
inscribed on a swing through San Francisco
some twenty years ago, that did that?)

Across the bay in Jack London Square this
morning, the refrigerated Southern Pacific
railway cars and eighteen-wheel semis were
unloading broccoli, spinach, cauliflower,
oranges and grapefruit, vast red slabs of beef
marbled with white fat, sides of pork, lamb,

chickens plucked and clean, twenty kinds of Chinese vegetables, tropical fruits I could and couldn't identify, Oregon blackberries and Washington raspberries, fifty varieties of cut flowers, Idaho potatoes. Clickety-clack, people were talking up a storm in English, Vietnamese, Spanish, Portuguese, and Chinese, and here on shaved ice in metal bins were a dozen kinds of ocean fish, their big, glazed eyes gazing at stalls stacked high with colorful melons of every size from a softball to a beach ball. I ducked into a breakfast café no bigger than our kitchen back in Vermont. Out came my notebook. Steinbeck could have pulled a short story out of Jack London Square before ten o'clock this morning. Likewise Jack himself.

Here's Harold, scribbling away at a tippy table in a hole-in-the-wall breakfast joint, in my Red Sox Nation jogging sweatshirt and coffee-stained khaki jogging pants, low-cut ratty sneakers, and sweaty Sox cap. He is as yet unshaven, unbathed, and suddenly quite undone, as the counterman hollers over at him, "Hey! You there. You hungry?"

"Well, maybe in a few —"

Outside the café, two young forklift drivers were racing their loaded machines down the crowded sidewalk as hard as they could go, devil take the hindermost. I was chronicling their contest in my notebook.

The counterman's sharp eyes took in my seedy appearance.

"What are you writing?" he said.

"Oh, just some notes. Maybe for a book."

"Right," he said. "Everybody's writing a book these days. I'm writing one. You know how to sweep?"

"Sweep?"

He came around from behind his counter, walked fast to a little closet, and returned with a push broom. He shoved it at me handle-first. "First you sweep. Then you eat."

The kindly counterman had assumed, not without good reason, that I was homeless (close), unemployed (closer), perhaps slightly deranged (on the verge), and *lacking the price of breakfast.* As in fact, having left my wallet back at the motel, I was. Naturally, it followed that I would claim to be a writer.

Fine. I swept the floor. It didn't take long and I was actually proud of myself. Fleetingly, I imagined a whole new career, my first honest-to-goodness real job in the real world in thirty years.

The counterman slapped down in front of me a paper plate heaped with gleaming fried eggs, several strips of crispy bacon, homemade toasted bread, and strawberry jam. He handed me plastic tableware and a large, steaming, paper cup of delicious coffee. I enjoyed every bite, then offered to mop the floor.

"No, thanks," said the counterman. "You can move along now and write your book. Somewhere else, not here. Goodbye. Good luck."

"Good luck with your book, too," I said, and headed out the door. Jack would have been proud of me, I thought. He'd swept a few floors in his day, too.

35
PORTRAIT OF THE ARTIST
AS A YOUNG DOLT

My short stint as a sweeper in Jack London Square wasn't my first foray into the janitorial field. For Christmas money in 1964, I took a temporary evening job at a downtown five-and-dime store in Newport, ten miles north of Orleans, at the south end of Lake Memphremagog.

Every day after school I parked our station wagon in the lot beside the frozen lake and made a dash for the store with the north wind howling at my back, blasting right out of Canada and producing a chill factor that would make International Falls in January seem tropical. My part-time night job consisted of general clerking, stocking shelves, unloading trucks, sweeping the old hardwood floor, and cleaning the restrooms, all for the princely sum of $1.25 an hour. The store was failing and slated to close right after the holidays. My aging boss was testy and didn't like schoolteachers.

It's Christmas Eve. There's a raging blizzard outside, what in the Kingdom is called a Canadian thaw — four feet of snow and a hell of a blow — with hordes of last-minute shoppers tracking in mud, slush, and snow. I'd swab out the restrooms, and half an hour later they'd look as if Attila the Hun and his outfit had just availed themselves of the facilities. Every hour on the hour I repaired to the janitor's closet to fetch the store's single push broom. An even more feckless predecessor of mine had managed to snap off so much of the handle that it now measured slightly under two feet long. To shove it along in front of me, I had to bend way over at the waist, which delighted my boss. He began to call me Igor of the North. Over the years the horsehair bristles had curled back like gnarled fingers. If, at the end of an aisle, I turned to survey my handiwork, I'd see a diagonal line of dust, lint, sidewalk salt, and indeterminable debris that the ancient, crippled push broom simply would not pick up. My sadistic employer would chuckle. "Mr. Teacher Man," he'd say, "you're leaving a trail. Do it again. Then get onto those restrooms. They look like hell."

What would Philip Marlowe do? What

would Jesus do? What in the name of heaven would *I* do if one of my students happened in and saw me, like Roger Miller's King of the Road, pushing broom at this dump? On Christmas Eve, no less. No sooner had that unsettling thought come to me than Prof himself stumbled through the door, three sheets to the wind and tacking down the aisle toward me like a derelict freighter headed for the breakers. "Mosher," he shouted, "you've got to lend me five dollars so I can get my wife a box of Christly candy. I forgot it was Christmas."

"I can't, Prof," I said. "Not until I get paid. Can you come back in a hour?"

"No, I can't come back in an hour," Prof roared. "In an hour I'll be passed out. You've got to help me."

I looked beseechingly at the store manager. He smiled and held up his index finger: one more hour to go. No advance.

"Prof, I'm sorry," I said.

"Goddamn you, Mosher," he shouted. "I thought you were my friend. You should clean shithouses for a living. It would do you a world of good."

With that he headed back out the door — but for once in my life, I thought of the perfect rejoinder right on the spot.

"Prof," I called after him, just before he

plunged into the raging blizzard like Lear himself, "I already do!"

36

The Parable of the Reluctant Samaritan

FROM *THE APOCRYPHAL GOSPEL OF BOB*

Now it came to pass that HAROLD WHO and the WEST TEXAS JESUS, out cross-country joyriding, journeyed up through the land of microbreweries and vineyards and good independent bookstores, past white-capped Mount Shasta, and into that region called Oregon. And here they paused to refresh themselves at a place of rest where there were outdoor faucets gushing rust-colored water, chained-down picnic tables, and brick facilities, both for men and for women, of which HAROLD had much need to avail himself.

And as our self-styled scribe came forth from the place of ease, a great clamor arose from a hard-used station wagon that had stopped near the Loser Cruiser in the parking lot — a clamor not of timbrels and lutes, but of a much anguished voice crying out, "Bob! Bob! Take me to fucking Roseburg, Bob."

And another voice, very wroth, shouting, "I ain't taking you nowhere, you no-good drunken son of a bitch."

And behold, two men conducteth an affray, one inside the station wagon and well stricken with years, the other in the prime of his manhood and as tall as the cedars of Lebanon, who sought to pull the thrashing ancient out of the front seat.

And the tall man saith, in a voice as loud as the ram's horn on the day of reckoning, "I don't care if you are my brother-in-law. Get out of my car, you COCKSUCKING BASTARD." And he would fain beat the rheumy-eyed elder, who wished nothing more than to be carried to Roseburg, and he did lay upon his shoulders and head many thudding blows, whilst a goodly number of wayfarers stood about, and were mazed, and knew not what to do. But one man in a semi hauling Douglas fir logs got on his CB and called 911 as the beating proceedeth.

Then spake the WEST TEXAS JESUS to that craven HAROLD, saying, "Best get your ass down there, boy, and put a stop to that business."

"Hurry up," added my uncle. "Otherwise that's going to end badly."

Otherwise? I was utterly persuaded that it

was going to end badly whether I intervened or not. The only difference was, if I got involved, it could only end badly for *me*.

But the battle did rage on, and "Take me to Roseburg, brother Bob," wailed the old man in the car, and he did cling to his sloshing bottle of WILD TURKEY with one hand and the steering wheel with the other, for he was much loath to be pulled out of the car of BOB. Who, in a towering rage, seized the elder's cardboard suitcase and strewed its sorry contents galley-west over the parking lot. But when BOB bent over to take his brother-in-law's leg and draw him out, the old rip's foot snapped up and struck him full in the nose, causing BOB'S LIFEBLOOD to gush forth.

"What are you waiting for, that big fella to kill him? Get on down there," the Undocumented Jesus said and, though much affrighted, HAROLD WHO ran toward the station wagon, not like the roebuck running to the doe at break of dawn, nor yet the fleet-footed Jacoby Ellsbury of the Boston Red Sox stealing second base, but he got there soon enough, and, NATURAL CRAVEN though he was, interposed himself between the loving brothers-in-law and lifted his hands in a placating manner and said, "Gentlemen, please. Is there some way

I can be of assistance here?"

Whereupon BOB, with his bloody nose still flowing copiously, said, "Yes, you can help me drag this son of a bitch out of my car."

At which the elderly brother-in-law rared back and hurled his now empty Wild Turkey bottle at BOB, narrowly missing HAROLD's head.

Minor Regional Writer Killed in Drunken Melee at I-5 Rest Area

Ooo-ahh, oo-ahh, oo-ahh, waileth the sirens of the police cars summoned by the Doug fir trucker. "Are you tied in with this outfit in the station wagon?" the first cop to arrive asked me.

"Never saw them before in my life."

Wild Turkey, however, pointed right straight at me and shouted, "He said he'd take me to Roseburg, officer."

The cop frowned. "You sure you want to do that, buddy?"

Off to the side, the Jesus of West Texas was nodding vigorously. I knew exactly what he was thinking. Not only did the Samaritan in *his* parable pick the robbed man up out of the road and clothe him in his own raiment and set him on his ass, he took him to the nearest inn and paid the innkeeper in advance for extended care.

Yes, yes, mouthed the nail-driving, pedal-steel-playing, unemployed Jesus, hands extended palms up, imploring me as if my very salvation hinged on driving this old sociopath up to Roseburg.

"I'll pass," I told the cop.

"Good choice," he said in his most official-sounding voice, and here, believe you me, endeth the Parable of the Reluctant Samaritan, from *The Apocryphal Gospel of BOB.*

37
SEARCHING FOR A VOICE

As a teenager, I fell in love with Hemingway's early stories, set in upper Michigan. To this day I would rate them among his best work. Like many another young writer, I tried, self-consciously and futilely, to imitate Hemingway's inimitable style. For several years the sentences in my sad little shoot-'em-up Westerns and baseball and fishing stories were clipped-off sound bites, five or six words long. Except for their brevity, these snippets had no more in common with Hemingway's prose than with Sanskrit. Midway through my junior year in college, I was rescued from my slavish emulation of a writer who has never been successfully emulated by my devotion to another novelist. William Faulkner was totally different from Hemingway in his approach to writing, but after reading *Light in August,* I became a lifelong Faulkner fan. Predictably, my own sentences began to lengthen out.

By the end of the semester, a short one was a hundred words long.

In my senior year at Syracuse I took the only creative writing class of my career. I had a good and sympathetic teacher, one who had already published several prize-winning stories and a novel. For these admirable attainments, not to mention his tremendous popularity with students, he was denied tenure and summarily discharged at the end of the year. The fact that he was, so far as I know, one of only two Jewish professors in Syracuse's relentlessly Waspish English Department may have been regarded as a black mark beside his name. At any rate, he was a fine writer, a fine teacher, and a fine guy, who has long since far exceeded the literary accomplishments and reputations of his mean-spirited former academic colleagues. During the winter of 1964–65, while I was teaching at Orleans High and going through an especially bad patch in my writing apprenticeship, in which I'd produce one five-word sentence like Hemingway, followed by a five-hundred-word sentence like Faulkner, my former professor wrote to assure me that if I persisted, I'd come up with my own voice. Night after night I kept struggling to do so, while I wracked my brain each day for ways to keep the kids I was trying to teach "out of the mill."

Like the off-again, on-again furniture factory back in Chichester, the Ethan Allen furniture mill kept Orleans alive economically. Not unionized, Dickensian in its working conditions, slouching between the river and the railroad tracks like the infamous nineteenth-century textile mills of southern New England, it was, by all accounts, a horrible place to earn one's living. Parents of backsliding offspring held up working at the mill as a fate worse than jail. Night and day, from inside our apartment across the river, we could hear the whirring blowers on the factory roof. Their perpetual low thrum was a constant reminder of the mandate we'd been given. "Keep the kids out of the mill, keep the kids out of the mill," murmured the big tin ventilators hunkered down on the factory roof like gargoyles, in the same part of my mind where I sometimes heard Huck Finn talking. But never the voice of my own that I was desperate to find. "Keep the kids out of the mill," said the blowers when I sat down late at night and tried to write the stories of our new home. "Out of the mill," chanted the blowers the next morning as I mogged off down School Street toward my day job.

Soon after the first of the year, at the advice of Prof, Phillis and I took a tour of the mill. Powdered with sawdust from head to toe, gray-faced, half-deaf, often minus one or more digits, lung-shot workers not fifteen years our senior looked ancient as they worked fast, fast, fast, doing piecework on shrieking saws, whining planers, roaring drills, and screeching edgers for wages that made my pathetic teaching salary seem princely. After the tour, "Keep the kids out of the mill" acquired a new urgency for us. But as the Kingdom winter arrived in earnest, the ever-present admonition of those blowers — I could actually hear them in my sleep — began sending me an urgent personal message. I loved working with the kids. I loved reading to them, talking to them about books, telling my ridiculous Bad Boy stories, reading the essays in which they poured out their hearts. Yet the harder I worked at teaching, the more evident it became that my heart wasn't entirely in what I was doing. Lord knows I tried. But to me teaching remained a road on the way to writing. Every day I heard more wonderful Northeast Kingdom stories crying out to be written. Yet I couldn't find the voice to write them in. Scribbling late into the night in our three-room garret, going to sleep every night and waking up every morning to the endless chivvying of those damnable blowers — "Keep the kids out of the mill" — I began to fear that it was not only my students who were in danger of tailing a ripsaw inside that inferno for the rest of their lives. If I couldn't teach and couldn't write, I might wind up there myself.

38
HARRY AND ME

Like the Bay Area of San Francisco, the "golden triangle" of Raleigh–Durham–Chapel Hill, and much of New England, the Pacific Northwest is prime book territory. The first Oregon indie on my itinerary was celebrating what was billed as Harry Potter's last hurrah tonight with a gala evening-long costume party, complete with a live owl, prizes, and discounts galore. In fact, the Harry Potter extravaganza had been cited as the main reason they couldn't host a Harold Who event this time around. Okay. I'd gladly defer to the likeable kid magician. After all, the income from his sales was helping to keep bookstores going so they could sell geezers like me.

Now let me emphasize that I am a huge Harry Potter supporter. Sure, the old schoolmaster within — the one I'd no doubt have turned into if I'd had the moral fortitude and common sense to remain in teaching — the schoolteacher within, I say, might *hope* that reading Harry at the age of eight or nine could lead J. K. Rowling's young acolytes to read *The Wind in the Willows* and the *Little House* books at ten and eleven. But most of the booksellers, librarians, and teachers I knew seemed to feel that *any* books that stimulated kids to read were worthwhile, and I agreed. For that matter, since leaving home, I'd seen a number of well-dressed grownups in bookstore cafés sipping lattes and poring over the latest Harry Potter as if it were the stock market report in the *Wall Street Journal.* And the more or less life-sized, scholarly looking, cardboard cut-out of Harry had met me at the door of nearly every bookstore I'd visited since Vermont — like a young Wal-mart greeter in a black gown. I'd read two or three of the books with considerable enjoyment myself. Harry is living, or almost living, proof that if you sit down and write a good, old-fashioned story well enough, readers, like the spectral ballplayers in *Field of Dreams* and the beneficent aliens in *Close Encounters of the Third Kind,* will come. J.K. did not need to attend Oxford's equivalent of an MFA program to learn that.

Parking downtown on this night of nights was a challenge. Right in the middle of the town square was a gaggle of celebrants — teenage girls in black lipstick, with hair the color of cotton candy striped as green as the outfield grass at Fenway Park, and guys loaded down with more chains than the ghost of Jacob Marley. Evidently they were forming up for a parade. The bookstore was just a few blocks away.

So Pa Kettle from Vermont sallies blithely up to a fifteen-year-old with a mostly shaven head crowned by a violet Mohawk and says, "Hi, there. Where are the owls?"

Blankness.

"The Harry Potter owls?" I said to the child nihilist. "You're here for the Harry Potter celebration, right?"

"Who the fuck is Harry Potter?"

With some degree of horror, I realized that this was *not* an innocent cavalcade of customers forgathering in honor of J.K.'s boy wonder. No. These were doped-up, disaffected street people, Goths, vagabonds of just the stamp I had been enjoined not to give my spare change to back in the New England college and resort town. Anyone else in the world except, perhaps, another writer, would have known as much at a glance.

Still, I was tempted to take a little impromptu exit poll, as I hurriedly made my own exit, to see how many of my anarchic young friends had read a Harry book. I'd bet at least half of them had.

The bookstore was jammed with kids and grown-ups, most of them in costume, even the adults. It looked like a set for the latest Harry movie. Or Halloween at Hogwarts. No, it looked like a Harry Potter party, nothing else. Dead-on Harry look-alikes, as humorless as little automatons, Hermiones by the dozen (though none of the masqueraders had quite captured the mildly androgynous affect of Rowling's young hero and heroine), bemused soccer moms in tall witches hats, warlocks and wizards, a little girl carrying a stuffed tabby cat with square markings around its eyes — that would be Professor McGonagall in her transmuted, feline form. And yes, dear God, a single live, rather bedraggled-looking great horned owl perched, untethered, on its handler's wrist near the door, regarding the goings-on with huge, enraged yellow eyes. The little girl thrust her stuffed cat at the owl, which spread its wings and hissed. "Wouldn't do that if I was you," the bird's handler said, with a leer. Wearing a shirt made from an American flag, he looked as though he'd just come off a twenty-four-hour shift as a ride operator at a traveling carnival about to go bust. The owl hissed loudly as the kid jabbed the pretend kittycat at it again. This bird was not the affable, reliable Hedwig from *The Goblet of Fire*. This was a deeply world-weary, irascible old raptor who, understandably, would rather have been anywhere else in the universe but here.

I slunk over to the fiction section for a shameless peek at the "M" shelf. No Howard Frank Mosher novels, but hey, this was Harry's day, not mine. Sidling up to our lad's cardboard likeness, I said, out of the corner of my mouth, "Congratulations. I guess you're selling a lot of books today."

"*She* is anyway," Harry replied.

"Just let me get this down," I said, going for my notebook.

The talking Harry nodded with the grim satisfaction of the chronically aggrieved. "That's right," he said, "and now she's up and killing me off. This isn't a book party. It's an execution."

"*Why?*" the little Hermione with the stuffed cat chanted, shoving the cloth feline at the agitated owl. *"Why why why?"*

"Why, *what,* Madison?" the mom in the witch's hat said.

"Why is that awful old man with the notebook *talking* to Harry?"

I looked around to see who little Madison

might be referring to. Surely she could not mean —

At that moment, the beleaguered owl lifted off its perch, seized Madison's cat in its talons, and swooped out the door and down the street. After Hedwig ran its carnie handler, with a bevy of begowned, skirling, shrieking Harrys, Hermiones, Snipeses, and Dumbledores hot on his heels. The roustabout handler finally caught up with Hedwig, who was mantling over the limp cloth cat on the village square. Madison screamed. Her mom struck out at the bird with her handbag. The flag-wearing owlman swore savagely. Unconcerned, perhaps unaware of the surrounding pandemonium, the Gothic street citizens passed bent little joints from hand to hand and reflected on the great void without and within.

"Look around," Harry said to me when I returned to the store with the other partygoers. "Look around and tell me one thing. Is this really what you want for yourself?"

I looked at the madding, book-buying crowd. I looked at the bustling young clerks (one of whom had told me, a few months before, when I phoned to try to set up an event, to use e-mail because it was, I kid you not, "much cleaner" — then of course never responded when I did). I looked at the feverish exchange of books, bills, and ringing coins. I looked at the soaring stacks of J.K.'s latest and at the kids with their bespectacled Harry and Hermione noses already buried deep in their purchases. Finally I looked back at Harry.

"Yeah, gov'nor," I said, "it is."

From a telephone conversation later that evening:

PHILLIS: So you're telling me, Howard Frank, that Jesus has returned in the incarnation of an illegal-alien hitch-hiker who wants to help you achieve commercial success and inner peace? And this same shyster all but got you beaned with a Wild Turkey bottle by telling you to get into it in a public rest area with an old drunk and his insane brother-in-law?

HFM: Bob.

PHILLIS: Bob?

HFM: The brother-in-law's name was Bob. The old man wanted Bob to take him to Rose—

PHILLIS: Howard Frank.

HFM: Yes?

PHILLIS: I rest my case. How's the new Harry Potter?

39
THE PACIFIC NORTHWEST

Back when hundreds of thousands of salmon a day would swim up the Columbia River past Portland in the spring, when the city was the stomping ground for a thousand roistering lumberjacks, it was known as Stumptown. Today the stumps are gone and roses grow everywhere. On my dawn run the next day, I found them twining up the sides of libraries and university buildings, leaning against rough riverfront taverns — pink, yellow, white, red as the sunrise, scenting entire neighborhoods. The orange blossoms of a clove-scented, twelve-foot-high climber adorning the sign of a concrete-block bail bond agency (EASY IN, EASY OUT) were as big around as a catcher's mitt.

Now that the stumps have been supplanted by American Beauties, Portland is also a city of books. Powell's City of Books happens to be the name of Portland's largest bookstore, which happens to be the largest independent bookstore in the country. Later that morning Bruce Burkhardt gave me a tour of this literary metropolis, where new and used books, hardcover and paperback, are shelved together by author, an arrangement that I, for one, like. He showed me the carved Oregon sandstone "pillar of books" that supports one of the store's entrances. Also the four-story-high skylight pouring sunshine down onto a shiny elevation marker set in the floor — 55.31 feet above sea level. Oh, and a manhole cover inscribed with a rose, beneath which, Bruce likes to tell rambunctious middle-school kids visiting the store, are three unruly thirteen-year-olds from a previous tour, still waiting for their parents to come get them.

Up in the coastal mountains of Washington I was struck by the strongest sense of being, well, at home. Of course, these mountains are two to three times as tall as ours, with snow on top year-round, but the maple trees and daisies and paintbrush, the fast, clear trout streams, and the lovely little off-the-beaten-track villages all reminded me of Vermont. And as the sun dipped into the Pacific and night settled over the vast landmass to the east:

WEST TEXAS JESUS: What was it you told me that writer fella said about driving after dark?

HFM: E. L. Doctorow? He said that writing a novel was like driving across the continent at night. You can see only as far as your headlights allow, but you know you're going to get there eventually.

WEST TEXAS JESUS: Who was that other old boy with initials for a first name? Jumped out of an airplane he'd hijacked up in this neck of the woods and disappeared off the face of the earth. Something something Cooper.

HFM: D. B. Cooper.

WEST TEXAS JESUS: That's it. Reason why I never set down my own stories? Back in the day? You ask me, writing a book's like jumping out of an airplane at night with a parachute you don't know how to open.

HFM: D. B. Cooper's an American legend, man.

WEST TEXAS JESUS: D. B. Cooper's dead. Fess up, now, Harold. Ain't that how you feel every time you set down to write a new novel? Like a man in free fall, with a big sack of money, a parachute, and no idea in the world how to open it?

HFM: Except for the sack of money and the parachute — yes.

40
THE LORDS OF MOSS

Like many another touring author, I never feel that a West Coast swing is complete without a visit to Village Books, Chuck and Dee Robinson's oceanside emporium of literature, ideas, and good fellowship in Bellingham, Washington. I love working cities, which Bellingham very much is, with a going fishery and wood-product industries. Also it's a jumping-off place, via ferry, for southern Alaska. Tonight I was slated to talk to a large (thank you, Village Books) group of readers about *my* corner of the country, three thousand miles away. And who's this? An early arriver, a dapper, self-possessed, middle-aged gentleman, his countenance fairly shining with anticipation. He was making for me with a very purposeful stride, waving — dear Jesus, no — that most dreaded of all documents a writer can receive, short of a subpoena from the grim reaper himself.

"Let me guess," I said. "You're a writer with a manuscript of a novel you'd like me to read."

"Wrong!" he gleefully shouted. "My name's Mosher, too. You're my long-lost relative!"

So, like that fabled little girl in the nursery rhyme, the one with the pretty little curl right in the middle of her forehead, when the Great American Book Tour is good, it's very, very good. And when it's bad — but no, that way lies cynicism. Suffice to say that it's not unusual for touring authors to encounter people sharing their last name, laden with genealogical charts and documents so deadly dull that by comparison an unpublished manuscript reads like *War and Peace.*

In the event, I got off pretty easily. Moshers, my newfound kinsman told me, are descended from Huguenots in Alsace-Lorraine. Inverted, the name Mosher means "Herr Moss" or "Lords of the Moss." In other words, my ancestors probably mucked around for centuries in the peat bogs of Europe. For all I know, the first Mosher scrabbled on all fours *out* of the peat bogs, having been spontaneously generated in the depths of the fen. But would Mr. Herr Moss, of the mossy-haired Moshers of

211

Bellingham, Washington, perhaps like to stay for my event? Not tonight, thank you. Tonight Herr Moss must get home to his genealogical research. If, however, I happened to have a box of complimentary copies of my new book in the car . . . Oh, soon enough, Cousin Moss, soon enough, the remainder bins would be overfl—. But let us not venture there tonight, when, absent Herr Moss, I have a full house at a great bookstore and am about to turn the corner and head east toward home and the love of my life — Mrs. Herr Moss? Frau Moss?

41
MARGERY MOORE

The winter of 1964–65 was a rough one in the mountains of northern Vermont. The Kingdom was hit with record snowfalls and then week after week when the temperature rarely rose above zero. One morning our outdoor thermometer read 50 degrees below.

One day in late January a thaw set in, melting the snow a little, but that night the temperature plummeted again. By the following morning the drifts in Verna's driveway had frozen solid, marooning us and our car with no way to get in or out. What's more, we were running low on kerosene, our sole source of heat.

A farmer on the edge of town owned a bulldozer, but when I asked if he'd plow us out he replied, in the grand old Northeast Kingdom tradition, "Why should I? You aren't from around here." So much for Vermont's help-thy-neighbor ethos. Help thy neighbor? Absolutely. But only if he's from Vermont.

"Call Margery Moore," another neighbor advised me. "She'll know what to do."

I'd already met Margery, a big, good-looking woman with friendly blue eyes, who owned a farm on the Willoughby River. In the fall Phillis and I had stopped to ask permission to cross her property to fish the river. "You young folks are welcome to fish or hunt here anytime you want to," she told us. "And if you ever need anything at all, just give me a shout."

I had no idea what Margery could do about our blocked driveway, but I called her anyway. "I remember you very well, Mr. Mosher," she said. "I'll see what can be done."

"Jesus to Jesus and seven hands around!" Phillis exclaimed ten minutes later. "There's a bulldozer plowing us out."

I never did learn what Margery said to the farmer who didn't like outsiders, but from that day forward the old coot couldn't do enough for us parvenu transplants from upstate New York, and neither could Marge.

Jim Hayford is who he is. Prof is who he is. Verna is who she is. I couldn't count the number of times I heard this phrase applied to the residents of the Kingdom during our first year in Vermont. More than anyone else I've ever known, Margery Moore is who she is.

Margery was and is famous — some might say infamous — throughout the Kingdom. First of all, she is famous for helping people. Like Ma Joad in *The Grapes of Wrath,* Margery never refused anyone a ride or something to eat or an encouraging word. Over the years she's taken in scores of homeless people of all ages, though she herself is poor and proud of it, her farm always teetering on the brink of failure. As a young teenager, she left home with all her belongings in a cardboard suitcase. She worked as a lumber-camp cook in Maine, a dance-hall waitress in Dodge City, and a horse trainer in Connecticut — Margie loves horses. She was the caretaker of a Long Island estate, attendant at a state hospital, dairywoman, forewoman on an airplane assembly line, hotel barkeep, and bouncer.

One evening when Phillis and I, still new in town, were walking past the tavern in the basement of the big wooden hotel at the end of Main Street, someone called out in a brisk voice, "Gangway, folks!" A woman in an apron appeared at the bottom of the steps, conveying, by the seat of the pants

215

and the back of the neck, a very large, very intoxicated patron whom she proceeded, without ado, to toss *up* onto the sidewalk. "All in a day's work," Margery told us, whisking her hands together. After I got to know Margery, I saw her, on two separate occasions, knock down rugged men. I've never heard her say an unkind word to or about anyone.

Though she loves all living things, and is as much of an unreconstructed romantic as anyone I've ever known, Margie was unlucky at love. Her first husband was given to "catting around." She left him high and dry in Dodge City. Back in Vermont, her footloose second husband got up from the breakfast table one morning, said he was going out to the barn to sweep down the cobwebs — and disappeared. Margie liked to tell us that for all she knew, the rounder was still at the barn sweeping cobwebs. In that same cheerful, matter-of-fact tone in which she'd called out "Gangway" before tossing the drunk up the tavern stairs, she informed us that she'd traded gentleman friends five times and "traded downhill each time."

Margery wrote beautiful poems about her travels and life on her hill farm. Once I saw her walk right up to a wild buck deer with her hands behind her back — "It's our hands they're afraid of; deer don't have hands." Another time I watched her call an eagle out of the sky. The bird lived with Margery for an entire summer. She named it Uncle Sam. Long before it was fashionable to claim Native American ancestry, she was proud of her Mohawk blood. She drove junk Cadillacs, Lincolns, and Chryslers. She was never on time in her life. She earned her high-school equivalency diploma at fifty and her paralegal degree at sixty-five. To save the expense of a dorm room, she slept in her car in the college parking lot, even in sub-zero weather. No one appreciated the irony of the law diploma more than Margie herself: although I have never met a more fundamentally honest person, she had long cultivated the image of a Northeast Kingdom Bonnie Parker, Belle Star, and Robin of Sherwood Forest rolled into one.

Like many Kingdom residents, Margie saw no reason to pay Vermont's unconstitutional poll tax. Incredibly, poll-tax delinquents lost their driver's license. For years troopers would stop Margery and ticket her for driving without a license. Not to be outdone, she kept in the glove box of her hundred-dollar Coupe de Ville or Continental a book of specially printed citations, and she'd ticket the arresting officer for driving on ancestral Indian lands without a proper license. Into court she'd sweep, with her waist-length glossy hair and snapping blue eyes. "A Vermont driver's license? There *was* no Vermont when *my* ancestors first came here. I thought the young officer was stopping me to ask for a date." Within moments she'd have even the most saturnine circuit judge laughing so hard he'd throw the case out the window.

Margery's mother died soon after she was born. By the time she was eight, she was doing most of the cooking, housecleaning, even keeping the farm's accounts for her dad and several hired men. One winter night she caught wind that the revenuers were on their way to raid her father's still. Not yet ten years old, Marge whipped up a batch of her famous molasses cookies and served them to the G-men hot out of the oven, detaining her guests until the old man had dismantled and hidden his still. Soon after I met her, she poached a well-fed doe in the next county over to help see her five children through the winter. She dressed the out-of-season deer in a man's overcoat, a scarf, and a slouch hat, then propped it in the front seat of her car with just the tip of its black snout sticking out between the scarf and the downturned brim of the hat. Sure enough, the game warden was waiting for her at the county line. Unable to find any evidence of wrongdoing after searching her car, he angrily asked why she was laughing. Had she been drinking? No, she said, but her "cousin," slouched up against the passenger door, had taken one nip of applejack too many. Whereupon the warden brusquely told her to get her drunken relative home to bed where he belonged.

A few weeks later, when the Orleans bank was robbed, the local constabulary went too far by fingering Margery as a "person of interest" in their investigation. It was time, she decided, to make a statement. First she marched into the bank and announced, in a voice loud enough to be heard two townships away, that she would very much *like* to rob it — this august institution had recently seen fit to turn down her application for a two-hundred-dollar loan — but she doubted that the bank had enough cash on hand to make it worth her while. The police stepped up their investigation and began appearing at her farm to question her at all hours of the day and night. It was time for phase two of our friend's plan. She hinted to a neighbor woman, a notorious gossip, that maybe she *did* know something about the bank robbery after all. And just maybe the loot was buried behind her barn under the towering manure pile that she'd wanted gone for thirty years but lacked the wherewithal to have moved. Only in the Kingdom (as Phillis might, and indeed did, say) would the cops fall for this ruse, showing up at the Moore place at three o'clock one morning with backhoe and bulldozer. Margie got her manure pile moved all right. At the bottom, the police discovered what one usually discovers at the bottom of a manure pile, and not one thing else.

42
THE HOWARD OF MOSES LAKE

MOSES LAKE the sign announced. THE OASIS OF EASTERN WASHINGTON.

On the day I arrived, the Oasis of Eastern Washington looked as arid as the Gobi Desert. I parked downtown and trudged through the most oppressive heat I'd encountered since leaving home — it was not yet 9:30 and already 100 degrees in the shade — into a small and blessedly air-conditioned bank to cash a traveler's check. While I waited in line for a teller, a man about my age came through the door, weaving a little.

"I'm here for my monthly withdrawal," he hollered.

"You can't make your withdrawal until the end of the week," one of the three tellers said with exaggerated patience, as if she were speaking to an overtired child. "You know that, Howard."

Howard?

"I need it NOW," Howard shouted. "N. O. W. I'm having a sugar attack. I have to buy my medication."

The trio of tellers looked at one another and rolled their eyes.

"Howard, Howard, Howard," the oldest teller said. "Come back on Friday. As you can see, we're very busy this morning."

This didn't seem right. They were denying this poor diabetic an advance on whatever stipend they were supposed to disburse to him?

"See here —," I started to say, but just then Howard looked at me and, I could have sworn, winked. In stentorian tones, he bellowed, "I'm feeling a spell coming on. Here she comes, here she comes. I'm going to loud up. Look out below, I'm going to fall down. I'm going to GET ROWDY AGAIN."

Maybe it was that "again" that did the trick. As the Howard of Moses Lake started to flap his arms spastically and lurch and stagger, the head teller capitulated.

"This is the last time, Howard. The very last time."

So it's five minutes later and I'm at the mini-mart next door, filling the thirsty tank of the Loser Cruiser. Standing at the clicking pump, daydreaming of cabbages and kings and my friend Howard, I noticed a new white three-quarter-ton pickup parked in the handicapped slot in front of the convenience store. On the shiny, outsized rear bumper, beside the license plate displaying the familiar wheelchair symbol, a sticker declared, I'D RATHER BE FISHING. That made sense. So would I. But as I replaced the nozzle and twisted the rusted gas cap back on, charging out of the store came, dear God, the Howard of Moses Lake. He was toting a twenty-four-pack suitcase carton of Bud, the King of Beers, in each hand. Without breaking stride, Howard heaved first one case, then the other, over the tailgate into the bed of the white pickup. Then he turned, winked at me again, and said, in the voice of a man who knows exactly how he is going to spend the rest of the day and, very probably, the rest of his life, "I got my medication. Now I can go fishing."

43
SACAGAWEA

How my uncle Reg would have loved the Howard of Moses Lake, I thought. Reg's unpublished and now missing history of Chichester had been full of colorful scamps, and I had no doubt that Howard would have fit right in.

There were ghost stories in my uncle's manuscript as well. My favorite began with the loud footsteps on the porch of the house where the ox driver John Everett had murdered his wife, Jenny, with an ax for a love affair she had not had. The footfalls — everyone in Chichester had heard them, even the village doctor — were believed to be those of the curiosity-seekers who gathered on Everett's porch after the murder, to view Jenny's bloody corpse through the front windows.

Like my storytelling uncle, I have always been deeply skeptical of, yet fascinated by, tales of the supernatural. Back in the late

1990s, when I was out west researching my Lewis and Clark novel, *The True Account,* I'd planned to see the famous fountain statue of Sacagawea at the junction of the Clearwater and Snake rivers, on the Washington-Idaho border. I missed seeing it on that trip, so this time I decided to swing down — it was no more than sixty or seventy miles out of my way — and pay my respects to the remarkable woman without whose assistance the greatest expedition of exploration in American history might well have ended in disaster somewhere in the Rockies.

Late in the morning I stopped at a pull-off beside the Clearwater to ask directions. Sitting on a grassy berm between the rest area and the river was an elderly Native American woman. She wore a plaid skirt and blouse, moccasins beaded blue and red, and a fringed shawl figured with elk, deer, and salmon. As I approached her, I realized that she was more than elderly. She was ancient. She was the oldest person I had seen since leaving home, perhaps close to one hundred, yet marvelously alive-looking, full of a serene vitality, with the kindest face imaginable.

"You're a long way from home," she said.

Had she spotted my green Vermont license

plate in the Loser Cruiser's rear window? I didn't see how. The Cruiser was tucked out of sight below the berm, and she was gazing out over the river in the other direction.

"About three thousand miles," I said. "But this is beautiful country."

We continued to visit for a few minutes. I asked about the local fishing, then inquired about the statue. My friend told me it was another mile or so to the west. I wondered, had she lived here all her life? Not yet, she said, like the old Vermonter in the story Mark Twain liked to tell. But her Nez Perce ancestors had lived in the area for, oh, ten thousand years or so.

Again I was struck by the light in her eyes and by her regal beauty. I've noticed that women who are especially kind often retain their beauty throughout their lives, but you can't really say that to someone you've just met, and judging by the care she took with her appearance, I was sure she knew it anyway. I thanked her for the directions and returned to my car.

The fountain statue was fully as striking as I'd heard. Unlike the older, rather heavy-set Sacagawea outside the capitol building in Bismark, North Dakota, this Sacagawea was a pretty, slender teenager. Water flowed over her fingertips, splashing into a basin.

And sitting beside the statue, looking out over the river, *was the elderly Nez Perce woman I'd met upriver.* The same figured shawl, plaid skirt and blouse, blue- and red-beaded moccasins. The same radiant beauty.

How did she get there? Did she fly, like the old woman who taught Blue Duck to fly in *Lonesome Dove?* Was she, perhaps, Sacagawea herself? Unwilling to demystify the experience, I returned to my car and headed north to my event in Spokane. Some stories should simply be left to stand alone, like the statue of that brave and beautiful young mother and American heroine, overlooking the junction of two great western rivers.

44
SPRING COMES TO THE KINGDOM, PART 1

My only other brush with the unaccountable took place during our first year in the Kingdom, at about the time spring began to creep north into the Green Mountains. The earliest harbinger of warmer weather in northern Vermont may be the shift in the blue jays' call from a harsh, hawkish cry to what the naturalist Roger Tory Peterson described as a "musical *queedle queedle.*" In 1965 the big, showy jays we fed in Verna's dooryard began their queedling in late February. A month later, when sugaring operations were in full swing in the maple orchards around Burlington and Montpelier, the Kingdom's sugar bushes were still locked tight in four feet of snow. By the second week of April, the sap had finally started to run up north. Once again, as on the first day of deer season, our classrooms emptied out. In that pre-plastic-pipeline era, farm kids were recruited to tap trees, lug sap buckets, and help with barn chores while their parents sugared off. Rose-tinted clouds of steam lifted high over the bare, black maple trees in the sunset. There were sugar-on-snow parties to attend, and wild bobsled rides down Allen Hill. My seniors and I read *Ethan Frome.* When we came to the tragic sliding accident, we talked about whether some people were trapped by their circumstances. I assured the kids that not one of them was trapped — and I hoped to Jesus it was true.

We went to "kitchen tunks" or "junkets" at the homes of our French Canadian students. While the sap boiled in the sugar houses, we danced and hummed and clapped the night through to the music of the champion fiddler Wild Bill Royer playing *"Sucre d'érable"* and *"L'église de Québec,"* often with a *Québécois grandmère* in the background accompanying on the "bones" — a pair of clacking dessert spoons. We feasted on *tourtière* and, though it wasn't Christmas, *Bûche de Noël,* the traditional frosted log cake, while grandmother told tales of the fearsome *loup garou,* the werewolf of the deep forest just over the border, who lured unsuspecting travelers to their deaths in the wilderness, and of the Three Ghostly Fishermen and the Little Blue

Virgin of Quebec. About half of our students could claim French Canadian ancestry on at least one side of the family. Perhaps a quarter still spoke French at home.

As spring approached, Phillis marched down to the Orleans slaughterhouse and returned with a few cow hearts and lungs for her biology class to dissect. She took her kids on expeditions along the Willoughby River and showed them how to identify skunk cabbage and wild ginger and bloodroot and coltsfoot and spring beauties. She helped them assemble entries for the county science fair and taught them the periodic table and how their own smart brains worked. My own teaching improved — a little. I was learning what to expect from my students, though I didn't expect Bill the brain to say, when I asked what they thought was the practical use of the stone wall in Frost's "Mending Wall" that divided the narrator's pines from his neighbor's apples, "Well, it might keep him from getting pineapples." Bill had just gotten a full scholarship to Middlebury. *Queedle queedle!* In general, the more I asked of the kids, the better they did. By dint of their own hard work, they were writing pretty passable essays on *Othello* and *Hamlet*.

Then came hopeful news of my own.

Coming down the stretch on my master's thesis on Shakespeare's villains, I learned that I had received a teaching fellowship to pursue my PhD in Elizabethan literature at the University of Pennsylvania.

Queedle? Why wasn't I more excited?

On the first day of trout season, with plenty of snow still in the woods, I assembled my fly rod and drove to a brook a few miles north of Margery Moore's farm on the Willoughby River.

I wasn't surprised to discover that my chosen stream was still frozen in places. It would be tough to cast, tough to avoid spooking the trout in the icy, crystalline water. But I tied a small red-and-white Coachman fly onto a light leader and headed upstream into the snowy forest, just as Dad and Uncle Reg and I used to do on opening day on the little mountain stream running down through Ox Clove into the ghost town of Chichester.

Though I had to creep along more like a hunter than a fisherman, stalking the few open pools so the trout wouldn't see me, I immediately felt the incomparable sense of well-being that I have experienced in the woods since early boyhood. In a stand of still-leafless poplars, I passed a cellar hole marked by a lilac bush not yet in bud. Nearby a Model A sat rusting on its wheel rims. Ages ago someone had tried to make a go of a farm here, then given up. But the little native trout were as lovely as ever, with emerald backs and flaming speckles, and even in the early spring of 1965, within a few miles of the new ski resort being built at Jay Peak, the only tracks I saw were those of a single river otter, which had fished up the stream a few hours ahead of me.

Suddenly I pulled up short, overcome by a sensation of foreboding. It came as unexpectedly as a thunderclap out of the still-wintery Vermont sky, and it somehow seemed to be connected with the murmur of the brook. At first I could not put a name to it.

I tried to continue fishing. But I was overwhelmed by a physical sickness, similar to the sickening horror that has come over me when I've seen old footage of World War II concentration camps. I hurried away from the stream toward a hardwood ridge, found a deer trail that eventually turned into an ancient lumbering trace, and just at sunset, came out on the road about half a mile from my car. Twenty minutes later, still shaken, I drove down the mountain toward Margery's.

45
Spring Comes to the Kingdom, Part 2

Margie ushered me into her kitchen for coffee. I told her about my eerie experience up in the woods, which reminded her of a tale about a first cousin whose home had been willed to her by an elderly maiden aunt. The place was rumored to be haunted by the ghost of a handsome young dress peddler who, during the Depression, visited Orleans for a few days each year and boarded with the aunt. The peddler, a natty dresser with flashy, two-toned shoes, drove a shiny black Model T Ford, new each year. One year he failed to show up, though for the past several months the aunt, wearing a different new dress each Sunday, had driven to church in a new Ford. The sheriff came calling, but the aunt was not one to brook impertinent inquiries. She smiled thinly and said that the peddler had left his car and wares with her and, assuring her he'd be back in a few days, had taken the train north to Canada. That was the last she'd seen of him. Time passed, and eventually the aunt herself passed, from her irreproachable status as a maiden lady to narrower confines in the resting place of her ancestors. As for Margery's cousin, some years after moving into the house she'd inherited from her famously straitlaced aunt, she removed a downstairs partition. Inside the wall she discovered a skeletal human foot and part of an ankle — in a two-toned shoe.

Some of Margery's tales were even darker. Not far from her farm, she said, a haunted house used to stand alone in the woods near a brook. When she was a girl, a couple from town rented the place but were frightened away by specters. Some years later, as Margery approached the empty house with a horse and wagon, she noticed a woman searching for something in the overgrown dooryard. As the wagon drew closer, the horse reared up and bolted. The woman vanished.

"He was a good, steady horse," Margery told me. "He never would have shied at the sight of a common person."

"This wasn't a common person?"

"It was the ghost of an alleged murderess."

Margery waited while I dug out my note-book.

"Her husband was a laudanum addict," she continued. "It was widely believed that one day when he was doped up, she took him out near the brook and killed him by pouring an entire bottle of the stuff down his throat. Some years later, the town fathers sent a local foster girl out to board with the woman and her grown son. My grandfather knew that the girl was being mistreated. More than once he'd seen her out doing chores barefoot in the snow. He reported the incidents, but nothing was done. A few months later the girl turned up dead."

"From what?" I asked, writing fast.

"Blows to the stomach. The coroner ruled that she was pregnant and had been killed by repeated blows to the stomach. Some-how, the woman and her son got out of it at the trial. But not long afterward the son committed suicide."

For the second time that day I felt sick, imagining the defenseless girl, the psycho-pathic woman, and her brutal son in that terrible remote place.

"After the son killed himself," Margery said, "the woman went mad. She spent the rest of her life ranting."

I thought for a minute. "From guilt?"

"Probably," Margie said. "But the form it took was unusual. She claimed that the sound of the nearby brook had become unbearable to her. First it made her sick. Then it drove her insane."

I sat forward in my chair. "What brook? Do you remember?"

Margery didn't know its name but offered to draw a map in my notebook. Painstakingly, she penciled in the mountain road leading north from her farm, the old haunted house, and the nearby brook.

It was the stream I'd fished that afternoon.

Just before leaving Margery's place that chilly April night, I asked a final question. "What was the woman's name? The supposed murderess?"

Margie told me. Then she shook her head. "I think who she really was," she said, "was evil personified."

46
BIG SKY COUNTRY

"I could spin a tall tale myself, back in my heyday," the West Texas Jesus boasted to me the next morning on our way through the mountains to my event in Missoula. We were following Clark Fork, one of the most beautiful trout streams in the West. My guy was eyeing it, spooling along in the valley a thousand feet below us through a series of deep green pools, white-water rapids, and trouty-looking runs of broken water.

"Back in your heyday?" I said. By now I wasn't sure whether he was talking about playing steel guitar and singing backup (he claimed) for Marty Robbins in a roadhouse in El Paso City, or telling stories from a mountaintop in Galilee.

Then, trouble. I'd been expecting it for the past week or so. It had been building day by day, and frankly, I was surprised that it hadn't come to a flash point sooner. Since Austin, Reg and the West Texas Jesus had been arguing, arguing about everything under the sun. Back in northern California, in a motel near Mount Shasta, they'd argued over whether the Catskills were true mountains or the remains of an eroded plateau. Reg said that the New York State history text he'd used with his kids at the one-room school in Chichester explained, in detail, that the Catskills were an eroded plateau. The West Texas Jesus said that for his money, a mountain was a mountain, period.

In Oregon, I'd spent the better part of an afternoon listening to them hash over the earth-shattering question of whether an eastern brook trout was a "true trout" or a char. Reg said a char. Jesus averred that a trout was a trout was a trout. On they jangled until I thought I'd go crazy.

This morning in western Montana, all of their wrangling came to a head over — baseball. That's right. Not religion. Not politics. Baseball.

What got them started was the old debate over whether a pitched baseball actually curved or only appeared to. (Dad and Reg argued interminably over this.) Reg took the affirmative and, while I think the West Texas Jesus probably knew better, he claimed that it was all an optical illusion.

"Get a bat," Reg said. "We'll settle this at the next ball diamond we come to." Jesus said he could put any pitch in Reg's repertoire "over the wall."

Since there was no way to settle this latest hoo-ha immediately, my traveling companions fell into a sullen silence. Below us as we continued east through the Rockies — at least we could all agree that *these* 10,000-foot-high peaks were not the remains of a plateau — the Clark Fork ran cold, fast, and clear.

"Let's wet a line," the West Texas Jesus said as we dipped down toward the river. "Pull into that fishing access, Harold."

"I've got a one o'clock in Missoula."

"We'll sink a six-pack in the river, fish up, and walk back down. Catch us some trout. Drink some ice-cold beer."

"I said, I have an event in Missoula."

"Fuck Missoula," said the West Texas Jesus, getting out of the car. "I'm going fishing."

"Wait!" I said. "I never did get to tell you about that unfinished business with my uncle."

But he was already headed down over the bank toward the river, six-pack in one hand, a fly rod in the other. A fly rod very much resembling the split-bamboo, seven-and-a-half-foot Orvis my grandparents gave me when I graduated from college.

I thought he called something over his shoulder as he started fishing up the river. I caught the words "about it." About what? I had no idea.

The last I saw of the West Texas Jesus, in the rearview mirror, he was tied into a good fish, his rod — or mine — bent and throbbing, his beer can lifted exuberantly, while the Loser Cruiser and I puttered on toward home and my reunion with Phillis.

47
MISSOULA

"About face!" I said on my way back to the Cruiser after my event that afternoon in Missoula.

Sitting on the sidewalk was a ragged young man with a pack of tarot cards fanned out in front of him.

"I'll give you five dollars if you'll answer one question for me," I said. "All you have to say is yes or no."

The five-spot seemed to vanish as I held it out toward him.

"Okay," I said. "I'm a writer. On a book tour. What I'd really like to do, though, is stay right here in Montana and fish for a week, then go straight home to my wife in Vermont. Should I?"

He scooped up his tarot deck, shuffled the cards, and spread them out on the sidewalk again, facedown. "Choose one," he said.

I should have anticipated this, but of course I hadn't. Truth to tell, those arcane tarot figures, up to God alone knows what devilment, have always spooked me a little. But I couldn't back out now. At least the cards wouldn't tell me I was going to come down with cancer. I'd already managed to do that on my own. Reluctantly, I pointed to one.

"Pick it up," the guy said.

Oh, Lordy. It was the seven of rods, a skeletal, malignant-looking bastard lugging seven sticks of wood on his back. Seven seven seven. Seven surgeries. Seven months to live. Seven Viagra prescriptions for radiation-related erectile dysfunction . . .

The reader took the card and studied it briefly. Then he said, "I think you've had a really bad setback at some point in your writing career that's made you wary of touring."

I couldn't help laughing out loud. "Man," I said, "like every writer I know, I have had *hundreds* of really bad setbacks in my career."

The tarot reader, no doubt sensing a kindred spirit in the charlatan standing on the sidewalk before him, said, "Finish your tour, buddy. It'll go fine. As for those other little matters you didn't mention" — and at that moment I would have sworn that, like the Howard of Moses Lake, he gave me a knowing wink — "no need to worry on those scores, either. At least not for a long time."

Oh, prescient Mr. Fortune-teller. Kind Mr. Fortune-teller. Even if you are a street-conning, scheming, lying-through-your-teeth Mr. Fortune-teller. Let me sign a book for you, give you the remaining two dollars in my wallet, erect a statue of you on the village green at home or right here in downtown Missoula, Montana. *Go fine. Other little matters. No need to worry.* Oh, happy afternoon. Thank you, thank you, thank you. "What do you think?" I said to Phillis on the phone that night. "Was he right?"

"He was," she said. "I could have told you that much for nothing. By the way, do you think your road bud will reappear?"

"The West Texas Jesus? Now that he's latched on to my fly rod, I doubt it."

"Howard Frank?"

"Yes?"

"You didn't really give your favorite fly rod to some old drunk who thinks he's Jesus, did you? On second thought, don't answer that. I love you, sweetie."

"I love you, too," I said.

That, gentle reader, was the one thing I

243

was sure of. But what more, really, could anyone hope for?

■ ■ ■ ■

PART III
LOVE

■ ■ ■ ■

48
Mr. Quimby
and Mr. F Nichols

Partly to clear my head so that I could make a sensible decision about the fellowship I'd been offered at Pennsylvania, partly to earn a few extra bucks, and in part to acquire some insight into a side of the Kingdom I wouldn't encounter in my classroom at Orleans High, I spent our spring break working for a neighbor, Mr. Aloysius Quimby. Mr. Quimby, a Northeast Kingdom jack of all trades, was a good-natured octogenarian religious zealot. He'd hired me to help him remove a gigantic dead elm that was bidding fair to topple over onto Jim and Helen Hayford's upper-story roof.

The third member of our strange little triumvirate was a raging alcoholic who lived in a round-shouldered school bus dating back to the 1940s. The bus had double layers of newsprint taped over the windows to keep out the light when he holed up, with several fifths of Seagram's Seven Crown, each Friday after work until Monday morning. Mr. F Nichols, as Mr. Quimby referred to him, had an unusual vocabulary, consisting principally of the word "fuck," delivered with an astonishing variety of inflections and sometimes prefaced or followed, for emphasis, by "yes" or "no." Thus the initial F, which Mr. Q came up with to replace Mr. Nichols's real first name, which I never did learn.

Throughout the Kingdom, Mr. Quimby was famous for a kind of surreal ingenuity. After spending a full day studying that behemoth of a dead elm, which loomed over the Hayfords' home at an angle that made the Tower of Pisa look plumb, he constructed a soaring trestle of disused railway ties between the tree and the house, a kind of brace for the first thirty or so feet of the elm's massive trunk to rest on while he severed the base with his chain saw. It took us a full week to build the trestle, which was the wonder of Orleans. Mr. F Nichols owned an elderly woods horse, with which he skidded the old railway ties up Cliff Street from the tracks below, where a half-mile section had recently been replaced. My job was to help Mr. Quimby hoist and lever them into place.

Mr. Quimby drove me to work in the

morning. His pickup was, as he described it, a "rig-put-together," a camelopard of a contraption that he had assembled from the bed and cab of a Model A truck, a 1952 Buick engine, and a homemade transmission. At eighty-eight, Mr. Q was as tough as a keg of ten-penny nails, but his joints stiffened up overnight, and for a few hours each morning, he was unable to turn his head more than a few degrees. He drove like a man wearing horse blinders. At the top of School Street, where just a few months ago — to me it now seemed like twenty years — young Cody had driven my car hell-for-leather backward on the first day of the semester, Mr. Q would stop and cut his eyes to the left to see what might be coming out of town on Route 58, which met School Street at a *very* dangerous, V-shaped intersection at the bottom of the hill. When all was clear he'd yell "Hang tight, Ezekiel!" and gun the rig-put-together down the hill like Dale Senior putting a rival into the wall at Daytona. On the third day I rode with him, we shot out onto the state highway directly in front of a loaded milk tanker. "Enjoy your fucking little ride with Mr. fucking Quimby, did you?" Mr. F Nichols inquired. From then on I walked to work.

"Ezekiel," Mr. Quimby said to me one

afternoon as we stood atop that insane trestle, surveying the village below. "It is a fine spring day in the Northeast Kingdom of Vermont, praise the Lord."

"It is," I said, wondering what the Lord would think of our outfit: a stiff-necked evangelist, a drunk, and a first-year school-teacher and would-be writer at a loss to know what to do with the rest of his life.

Mr. Quimby paused to mop his brow with his slouch hat, then looked off into the distance. "Behold the new green foliage, Zeke. Vermont's foliage, fall or spring, is as glorious a sight as any this world has to offer."

No argument there.

"But, Ezekiel, the splendors of this spinning blue sphere" — Mr. Q fancied himself something of a poet-orator — "are as naught to the glories of paradise. Where, by the by, I expect soon to be seated at the right hand of Him who shaped us in His sublime image."

"I hope not *too* soon, Mr. Quimby," I said, remembering that we had both come perilously close to exactly such a translation earlier in the week at the foot of School Hill. I could still hear that tanker's bleating horn.

Mr. Quimby chuckled knowingly, as if his friend on high had vouchsafed to him the exact moment of his celestial ascent.

"How about the Hayfords?" I said. "Will they be seated up there with you?"

Mr. Quimby gave this a moment's consideration. "James and Helen are good enough folks," he said rather cautiously.

At that point Mr. F Nichols appeared, sweating out his hangover, shouting fuck this and fuck that, repeatedly whacking the back of his overloaded horse with a makeshift cudgel he'd cut for that purpose. "What about him?" I asked.

"Not a chance in the world," Mr. Quimby said, and he clambered down off the trestle, yanked the cudgel away from the drunk, and sent it sailing end over end onto the neighbor's lawn. He said something quick and low to Nichols, then turned his back on him. To this day I don't know what Mr. Q told Mr. F Nichols, but at least on that job the guy never beat his horse again.

As for me, building that Babel-like monstrosity — it worked like a charm, by the way — with Mr. Quimby and Mr. F Nichols turned out to be another small but memorable part of my apprenticeship in the Kingdom. Still, trudging back to Verna's in the early evening, inhaling the sweet fragrance of varnish from the mill, I wondered. Did I really want to live in Philadelphia for three years? If not, what was I doing with my life?

D. B. Cooper had yet to hijack an airliner and leap into the dark sky over thousands of square miles of western wilderness. But as I drove south out of Missoula on Day Fifty of the Great American Book Tour, heading for an event in Hamilton and remembering our long-ago first year in the Kingdom, I understood what the West Texas Jesus had meant by comparing us callow storytellers to the flying bank robber who made his fateful plunge.

49
THE CONTINENTAL DIVIDE

This morning I was parked beside my favorite western trout stream, in southwestern Montana's Pioneer Mountains, contemplating the five hundred miles the Loser Cruiser and I still had to cover to make our engagement that night in Salt Lake City. Even by western standards, it seemed like a haul, though as Russ Lawrence chronicles in his lively history, *Montana's Bitterroot Valley,* the Native American ambassador Old Ignace *walked from the Bitterroots to St. Louis and back, on behalf of his people, not once but twice.* So I slid back behind the wheel and headed off through the Big Hole Valley at my customary 58.5 mph. Approaching the Idaho state line, I coaxed the Cruiser up to 70, hoping the speed might transcend the shimmying. Instantly, the entire front end of the car went into a deep grand-mal shuddering. Back to 58.5.

■ ■ ■ ■

It occurred to me, as I cajoled the old Chevy up the hill above the Babylonian-looking metropolis of Salt Lake City to the King's English Bookshop, that to a story-teller like me, Joe Smith's marginally more outlandish retelling of a wondrous old tale made a fine American yarn. With, what's more, an appropriately American capitalistic touch — Moses' tablets, after all, were made of mere stone. Joe's were pure gold.

The King's English, Betsy Burton's renowned independent on the ridge above the city, shares its name with Betsy's memoir of her life as a bibliophile and bookseller. One of her cardinal rules is "never host an event for a book you aren't passionate about." As I waited for my event, it struck me that the same precept ought to apply to writing a book. How many of the nearly half-million new books published or distributed in the United States each year would ever see daylight if writers wrote *only* those books they were passionate about? A well-behaved and attentive shepherd dog attended my talk that evening at the King's English. There were no after-dinner nappers. (At one venue in New England a guy had actually fallen asleep *before* my reading and slept soundly through it from beginning to end.) Thank you, Betsy. I'll be back.

This place they call Wyoming is one tough and beautiful country. You need only drive along Route 90 from Evander to Rock Springs to Rawlins, past tin-can horse trailers and cattle-sorting pens and railyards and petroleum pumping stations, past walking beams extracting oil with a dreary, seesaw monotony, past mile-long coal trains and interstate exchanges that look like sets for B Westerns, past bone-white alkali streambeds and grazing Angus and Shorthorns and Whitefaces and a few long-abandoned sod huts slumped into sidehills, and then, suddenly, profiled on a distant butte, a single antelope. Like the Kingdom, Wyoming seemed a good place for a man or woman of a certain sanguine temperament to live. And a hard, hard place in which to make a living.

So, like the cowboy in the ballad, I'm walking the streets, not of Laredo but of Laramie, which, with its squat brick utilitarian downtown buildings, looks like any other western town. I slipped up a flight of stairs that could have led to a Prohibition-era speakeasy or whorehouse — an impression enhanced when a Burlington Northern freight rumbled by not thirty feet away, shaking the building to its foundation — and into Personally Recommended Books (aka The Second Story), where, staring me in the face, was a display of my latest with a RECOMMENDED READING tag. Any writer will tell you — that's a moment worth the drive from Vermont to Wyoming.

Later, though, in Cheyenne, I was the only one on hand to admire the vase of freshly cut yellow and orange chrysanthemums beside my books on the signing table at City News & Pipe Shop, since by then it was raining too hard for anyone to venture onto the streets, with plenty of rolling thunder and great sheets of electricity lighting up that big western sky like the approach of doomsday.

That night, after dodging more cloud-bursts under a lime-green sky the likes of which I've seen between storms in Montana and once in a Charlie Russell painting but never back in New England, I bunked in at a rundown motor court next to a roadhouse, where I drank too many Silver Bullets. For weak-headed Harold, that's two cans. I lurched back to the Bates Motel, keeping a watchful eye out for Norman and his mother. I huddled on top of the bedspread,

fully clothed and wearing my Red Sox jacket
— I'd be damned if I'd climb in between
Mother Bates's gray sheets — and read
myself to sleep with Annie Proulx's *Close
Range.*

Wyoming, I thought, just before drifting
off. Tonight I was content just to be in
Wyoming.

50
THE GREAT NORTHERN
EXPRESS

Back in Vermont in the wintry spring of 1965, our lives got even busier. Sometimes we'd fall asleep over our lesson preparations, stagger to bed too exhausted to make love, wake up at three or four in the morning, remedy that, then up again at five — keeping farmers' and hunters' and, by God, *teachers'* hours. How did we do it? How does any teacher do it? I have no idea. And we were frequently reminded by Prof, now that negotiations for next year's salaries were under way with the school board, that we weren't even close to earning the $1.15 an hour we had calculated we were being paid. The hourly rate at the mill was $1.25, not counting piecework. "Keep the kids out of the mill?" I thought indignantly — maybe we should keep them out of teaching. Yet from watching Jim and Helen Hayford and Phillis, I knew that teaching, done passionately, was a noble profession. And soon it might be my profession on the college level. Or at least "something to fall back on" if writing didn't pan out. A poem Jim Hayford had written the fall before he graduated from college kept going through my head:

Senior Year

The fall wind touches the man who hoes
His upland garden clean for spring,
While faraway autos sing
And a faraway rooster crows.

The fall wind hurries the man who goes
On foot a stony village road
In the service of his Lord,
And hugs his cassock close.

The fall wind whispers to him who knows
Only the breathless air of stacks,
Tracing in ancient books
The roots whence man arose.

The fall wind searches out all those
Who feed man's body or soul or mind,
I ask it which it will find
Me doing when next it blows.

We continued to see a lot of the Hayfords.

259

Jim and I both loved trains, and often on spring evenings when it didn't happen to be snowing, he and Helen and Phillis and I would take a picnic supper over to the railroad station at the south edge of Orleans and sit on the wooden benches beside the track to watch the mile-long early evening freight go by. Out of Helen's wicker picnic hamper came fried chicken, thick slices of well-buttered homemade bread, oven-baked beans laced with this year's fancy-grade maple syrup. And for dessert, Phillis's no-egg chocolate wonder cake. Like many countrymen of his generation, Jim carried his round dollar watch in his trousers pocket and his change in a small black snap purse. He'd take out the watch and consult it with a judicious air, like a dutiful stationmaster. Soon we'd hear the train whistle at the crossing north of town, still far enough away to sound hollow and fluty, but when I put my hand on the rails, I could feel the deep vibrations of all those onrushing tons of steel. Away up the line, we'd see the Cyclopean light of the lead engine, brilliant in the twilight, accompanied by a louder, sharper whistle, then the first of four 100-ton diesel locomotives would pound by scant feet away, followed by 150 cars. Flatbeds loaded high with fresh lumber, tawny gold in the

260

mountain dusk, fragrant with resin. Canadian pulpwood bound for paper mills in Maine and New Hampshire. Grain from the Midwest. Alberta oil in tankers black as night, and oh, the stirring names on the sides of the cars: Santa Fe, Southern, Delaware and Ohio, Grand Trunk. And then, in the heavy silence as the train vanished into the dusky hills south of town, that lone, battered Great Northern "Express" boxcar would reappear on the siding across the tracks, reminding me of the day we first came to town, one year before.

That year I was on my own Great Northern Express, riding deep into the heart of this northern Kingdom on a train that, like those still barreling through Orleans in the '60s, had a bad case of Arlo Guthrie's disappearing-railroad blues. I needed to chronicle what I saw rushing by outside the window *right now* because soon it would be all gone. How could I possibly cut myself off from this gold mine of material before I'd even staked a claim and begun to pan the surface? How could we leave this "last best place" that almost despite ourselves was becoming home?

Then Margery Moore told me a story from her own life that framed my question precisely without quite answering it.

261

■ ■ ■ ■

Reeking of hot creosote and train oil and diesel smoke, with an occasional whiff from the nearby stockyards, the railyards of Dodge City sprawled out before me in the savage heat of the August afternoon. They must have looked much the same as in the mid-1940s (absent the steam locomotives) when a beautiful but heartbroken young woman, leaving behind a failed marriage, loaded onto a rented boxcar several cows, a flock of Plymouth Rock laying hens, a tall rooster with a flaming comb, a nanny goat, three sheep, a strutting tom turkey, a Morgan riding horse, two geese, and a very large and very pregnant sow. Then Margery Moore swung aboard herself and rode the rails east out of Dodge toward her true home in Vermont, some 1,800 miles away.

I know that at twenty-five Margery was beautiful because I have a picture of her at that age, posing with her handsome young husband at a Dodge City photo studio just a few months before her flight back to Vermont. I know she was heartbroken because years later, in the spring of 1965, she told me so. Still, she never wept, even once during the next ten days, as she shepherded her menagerie of farm animals through an uncertain connection in Kansas City, bullied officious freight agents in St. Louis and Chicago, joked with brakemen in Akron, gave half a dozen eggs to a half-starved hobo in Cleveland, watered her stock at nameless little junctions in western Pennsylvania, and fended off a railroad detective with an eye toward an impromptu romantic interlude on a siding in Buffalo. She arrived in Orleans just in time for the blizzard of the century. Commandeering a cattle truck from the local auction barn, Margery drove her animals three miles east to the Moore family farm, then led the horse, cows, and other four-footed critters half a mile through waist-deep snow to the barn, carrying the turkeys and chickens and geese over her shoulder in feed sacks. Not until dawn, with the wind howling like the mythical *loup garou* that had terrorized her Native American ancestors and the sow birthing the first of thirteen piglets, did Margery finally break down and cry. She was home.

51
THE GREAT PLAINS

On I went, through the tall-as-an-elephant's-eye cornfields of Dorothy and Toto's Kansas, suffused with the hot, gritty scent of corn in full fruit. Past ten-mile-long fields of grain being harvested by ten-ton green combines that did everything but bake it into bread. I flushed lemon-breasted Western larks — with their short wings and shorter tails they scarcely looked aerodynamic — and yellow-headed blackbirds from storm ditches and rest-area dog walks. Then, right on the Nebraska state line, I saw my first-ever giant swallowtail butterfly. At sixty-five, that's a splendid thing to be able to say.

When my great-grandfather Eugene Hart was a very old man, he made a pilgrimage by train from upstate New York to Nebraska to visit a boyhood chum who'd come west decades earlier. They tottered over the friend's section of rich, black-dirt farmland, took a gander at the sod house he'd lived in for his first five years in the territory, then sat out on the porch together after supper for a couple of hours without speaking a single word, since they were both as deaf as fenceposts. At the end of the evening, Great-Grandpa's friend nodded, stood up, and shouted in my ancestor's good ear, "Gene, aren't we having the grandest visit in all the world?"

And I love the way small cities on the plains loom suddenly up out of the level landscape, their two or three modest downtown skyscrapers shimmering in the late-summer heat. Once the blue-eyed grass covering the unbroken prairie in these parts would snag in the curved horns of the sodbusters' oxen, as it had in the spurs of the buffalo hunters before them. Today the people those hunters and farmers dispossessed are clerking at casinos. The remaining buffalo are low-cholesterol curiosities, as docile as steers milling in a feedlot. Our Great Plains, too, are somewhat diminished, but I wouldn't have missed seeing them on this trip for the world. I wouldn't have missed any of the sights and experiences my journey had afforded me. The first human beings to pass this way heard messages of great import in the eternal winds sweeping over the prairie. Perhaps the wind and the songbirds and the dwindled bison herds had a message for me, if I could slow myself down long enough to hear it. Maybe that *was* the message. *Slow down. Enjoy every minute in this lovely rolling land of yellow-headed blackbirds and giant swallowtails. Enjoy it and then, like your friend Margery, find your way home.*

Only after I returned from the Great American Book Tour did Phillis confide how worried she had been about my launching out on such an extended journey so soon after my radiation treatments. She said that each night when I called her, she was relieved that I'd made it through another twenty-four hours and was one day closer to home. As usual, she had understood me better than I'd understood myself. All along I had conceived of this trip as something I wanted to do. Phillis, despite her unspoken concerns, realized that it was something I *needed* to do.

But what, you may be wondering, was she doing back in Vermont while I was plying the highways, canvassing the independent bookstores of America? In early June, when I'd set out on my trip, Phillis was in the flurry of the end of the school year. A decade before, she had become increasingly aware that many of her students had serious personal needs that were interfering with their learning. In her mid-fifties she returned to graduate school and, working nights, weekends, and summers, earned an MA in counseling. As a school counselor, her work week lengthened from the ordinary sixty or seventy hours most teachers put in to something like one hundred, many of which were spent helping parents and other teachers help the kids.

World-class caregiver that she is, Phillis was also, that summer, helping my wonderful ninety-year-old mom live independently in an apartment just up the street; attending students' baseball games, motocross dirt-bike races, and, in consequence of said races, hospital bedsides; tending our gardens and apple orchard; answering my e-mail; and searching for Monty, her six-foot-long ball python, who had squeezed out from under the lid of his cage and, she feared, gotten into the school's heating ductwork.

Years before, Monty had appeared out of nowhere in the middle of a neighbor's lawn, an unclaimed escapee. Phillis gladly adopted him. In time, not a child at her school was afraid of snakes. Indeed, the kids came to love Monty. Not so the school principal and several teachers.

That night, from a lonely little motel on the Great Plains, I asked Phillis if Monty had turned up. Not yet, she told me, but she was confident that he would.

"Couldn't you call him? Like a dog? He seems to like you a lot."

"Snakes don't have ears. He'll show up when he's thirsty."

Dear Jesus. I'm not in love with snakes myself. I envisioned Monty shouldering aside a tile — do snakes have shoulders? — in the ceiling of the principal's office and leisurely extending two or three feet of his cream-and-brown snaky self down, down, down to peer, split tongue flickering inquisitively, into the principal's face.

"You're a lucky one, Harold," a raspy voice in the prairie wind informed me after I turned out the light.

Him again.

"To have a gal like that Phillis," he explained.

"I know it," I said. "How about you? Ever married?"

"Only four times," he said, and then there was a *snap,* like a cap being popped off a bottle, and then there was just the wind.

52

READING THE HEARTLAND

When Vivien Jennings was a little girl, visiting her grandparents' red-clay farm in the hills of Arkansas, she discovered a handsome, bronze-colored snake behind her grandfather's barn. Always an adventurous kid, she picked it up and began to play with it, slipping the reptile in and out of an empty Hellmann's mayonnaise jar. When she showed her grandparents her find, they were horrified. Vivien's new playmate, it turned out, was a poisonous copperhead.

To me, the copperhead story reveals a lot about this well-known civil rights activist turned world-class bookseller. Vivien and Roger Doeren, her partner at Kansas City's Rainy Day Books, recommend titles to 150 area book clubs. Rainy Day Books cosponsors scores of events each year with local libraries, restaurants, and community service groups. Vivien or Roger attends every author function. "If writers honor us by coming, we want to be there for them," she told me on the day after I saw the giant swallowtail in Nebraska.

After my reading, Vivien and Roger took me out for supper at the Bluebird Bistro, where they'd recently cohosted an event for a cookbook author. Over fresh rainbow trout and a garden salad grown in the lot across the street, the conversation turned to handheld electronic readers. Would they, I wondered, eventually replace books?

Roger grinned. "Has anyone ever asked you to sign one?"

"Books don't need batteries," Vivien said. "You can get sand on them. And" — she smiled, and for a moment I could see in her eyes that venturesome little girl, barefoot on a backcountry Ozark farm, with the deadly serpent in the Hellmann's jar — "books work. One hundred percent of the time."

Midnight in a motel in Kansas City. Paying dearly for that salad (try going six months without a fresh tomato) but not regretting it. Taking inventory: one (1) twenty-year-old Chevy Celebrity; two (2) author interviews slated for tomorrow in St. Louis (during a recent radio interview in Denver, the host had introduced me as Chris Bohjalian and asked what it had been like to go on *Oprah*);

three (3) book events to do in the next two days; four (4) good novels on my bedside table; and five (5) imponderable questions that had just popped into my head:

1. Why isn't man ever called the reading animal? After all, isn't reading the one thing, in addition to causing mischief for its own sake, we can say, with assurance, that we do better than manatees, armadillos, and pangolins?
2. Why isn't Jesus ever reported as reading *anything?* "It is written," he loved to say. When did he do his reading? Why didn't I think to ask him before he jumped ship back in Montana?
3. Why hasn't Vivien Jennings (or another great independent bookseller) won the Nobel Peace Prize? Aren't independent booksellers the last public guardians of our human rights and, along with librarians and teachers, the keepers of our cultural and literary traditions?
4. Why is it that, in a rundown motel on the outskirts of Kansas City, with the witching hour upon me and a fried gizzard, running to the

can every six minutes, a large bottle of Kaopectate in hand, because I had the temerity to eat that tomato — why is it that I'm about as content as a touring writer can be? I can answer that. It's because in the *other* hand, the one not grasping the Kaopectate, I'm holding Richard Russo's novel *Bridge of Sighs,* and I can't remember when I've met a more likable and compelling townful of folks in any book since Russo's own *Empire Falls.*

5. Which reminded me. What *was* the name of that Depression-era conman novel I read and loved and gave away thirty years ago and have been searching for, like the Holy Grail, ever since?

"The book is dead, long live the book," I said aloud. "Goodnight moon. Goodnight man with the red balloo—"

That's not funny, Harold. That's just silly. Go to sleep.

Still hunting for that maddeningly elusive novel the next afternoon in the fiction section of the St. Louis County Library, where I'd be speaking that evening, I found myself remembering some of the high points of my personal history as a library habitué. I remembered exactly where I was sitting in the library of our small-town high school, the slant of light over the baseball field outside the window, even the time — it was 10:20 a.m. on the big, round Seth Thomas library clock — when I first read D. H. Lawrence's great short story "The Rocking-horse Winner." And the very chair at the very table in the reading room of Syracuse University's now long-demolished old library where, on my second time through, I realized that Faulkner's *Light in August* was a masterpiece. Not to mention the Saturday afternoon in the periodical alcove at the village library in Orleans when I picked up the latest *Atlantic Monthly* and suddenly it was an hour later and I'd read the entire long excerpt from James Dickey's *Deliverance* without moving an inch. "Mr. Mosher, are you all right?" the librarian finally asked. And right here in this library in St. Louis a few years ago, I read the first few chapters of *Undaunted Courage,* standing like a sleeping horse or a catatonic writer in front of the new nonfiction display near the main desk. Reading.

Then there was the spring afternoon in 1965, during my first year as a teacher, when I harried my juniors into the school library to acquaint them with the Dewey Decimal System. With which, it must be said, Harold Who had only the slenderest acquaintance himself. We'd no more than started when, out of a little hedgerow of chokecherries bordering the deepest part of center field on the school baseball diamond, stepped a small deer. Up shot Little Prof's hand. "Mr. Mosher, Mr. Mosher! Can I get my bow out of Dad's car and shoot that deer?"

Now, I hereby invite any of my readers who have ever taught high school kids in a rural area to tell me what I should have said. Admittedly, what I probably should *not* have said — hunting season having ended months ago — was, "Sure, L.P. Just be careful to check your background. Don't shoot any first-graders."

Little Prof was already out of the room. Two minutes later, with the deer now grazing behind second base, I saw him sneaking around the corner of the school, bow in hand like Natty Bumpo, just as, dear Jesus, the library door opened and, stumbling into the room in all his red-faced glory came Prof himself, flush from a two-quart day and intent on conducting a teacher observation.

"Stand down, boys and girls, stand down. Continue as before," bellowed the old educator, dropping into a chair, his clipboard and pen at the ready.

"So," I said, trying to position myself between my semi-intoxicated employer and the window overlooking the ball field, "we will turn now to the 500's and biography . . ."

"Mosher," Prof said, craning his neck. "Is that my boy out there?"

"Out where, Prof?"

"Out in the school yard, you dumbbell. Stalking that Christly little skipper."

I pretended to scan the ball diamond. "Oh, no, I don't think —" By now Little P was within range. Arrow nocked, he raised the bow — and hurried his shot. The arrow flew harmlessly over the startled animal, which took three bounds and vanished into the hedgerow.

Prof shook his head. "Buck fever," he said. "I just don't know about that boy."

And, forgetting all about evaluating me, he wandered out of the library and repaired to his office to commiserate with himself over a third quart.

53
CHICAGO

We sell books the old-fashioned way . . .
we read them.
— ANDERSON'S BOOKSHOP,
NAPERVILLE, ILLINOIS

Chicago has the damnedest highway toll system in the United States of America. If you're on one of the numerous interstates crisscrossing the city and you don't have an Illinois freeway pass, you have to keep pulling off to throw quarters into an automatic collector. Like calculus, it's simple enough if you understand it. I didn't, and ran half a dozen toll booths before I realized what they were. Good work, Mr. Vermonter, and now for an appearance at a Chicago mall — how did I get roped into this? — next door to a strip joint with bars on the blacked-out windows. A neon sign read ONE NITE ONLY MISS FIFI FYRE AND LITTLE EGYPT IN *FIREROTICA*.

Judging by the numerous cars and pickups in the strip-joint parking lot that evening, the glamorous Miss Fifi and Little Egypt had a good turnout for their brief stand in Chitown. Nearby at the mall bookstore, I did not. Two people showed up: Harold Who and the store manager, who was in a white heat to close for the evening and get over to catch *Firerotica.*

"E-GYPT. LIL EGYPT. YOU LET ME IN THERE, GIRLFRIEND. IT'S FIFI."

I started upright. A rain of blows fell on the door of my motel room, accompanied by more injunctions to let my nocturnal visitor *the fuck into the room or else.*

I staggered to the door, which seemed ready to pop off its hinges. Thank God it was just my prostate gland and not my heart that was at risk. Shades of Miami and the [B]udget In[n].

"Excuse me," I called out, as if *I* were the one waking up half the city of Chicago. "Excuse me, ma'am. This is 202. Howard Mosher? I'm afraid you have the wrong room."

"ROOM SCROOM. LET ME IN THERE, GAL, OR I GONE KICK YOUR LYING ASS ALL THE WAY TO *DE-TROIT.*"

I opened the door. There, in some kind of skimpy terry-cloth getup, stood (I judged) the celebrated Miss Fifi Fyre. "Say," she said. "You ain't Lil Egypt. You got my girlfriend in there somewhere, young man?"

It was that "young man" that did it. I began to laugh.

"I'm sorry," I said, still laughing. (Why was *I* sorry, for the sake of the West Texas Jesus?) "You really do have the wrong room."

Miss Fifi was up on her tiptoes, bobbing around and peering past me to see what I'd done with her sidekick.

"What's your room number?" she said.

"This is 202."

"Two-oh-*two?* Why didn't you say so? We're in two-oh-*four,* boy. I got the wrong room."

More laughter, this time mutual.

"Well," Miss Fifi said, "you go back to sleep now, Mr. Two-oh-*two.* Get your beauty rest. Ha."

"Sorry," I said again, and just before Miss Fifi began to beat on 204 with all her might, she waved back at me like a railway switchman giving the highball signal and called out, "No problem, dude. No problem at all."

54
Harry W. Schwartz:
The Bookstore That
Made Milwaukee Famous

In 1921 a two-fisted, fearless kid named Harry Schwartz, who had the ironclad sense of right and wrong of a Horatio Alger hero combined with a love of books and more than a touch of the iconoclastic exuberance of the young Mark Twain, hopped a freight in Milwaukee and bummed his way west to Los Angeles. He landed a job at a downtown bookstore, sweeping up and tending the nickel book bins on the sidewalk. For Harry it was love at first sight. Head over heels, he fell for the bookselling business.

A few years later, Schwartz returned home to Milwaukee and established Casanova New, Old and Rare Books, stocked initially with books from Harry's personal library. Over his long, illustrious career as an activist bibliophile, Schwartz championed the early work of Faulkner and Hemingway, fought tooth and nail against every kind of censorship, risked going to jail for selling banned novels by James Joyce and Henry Miller, raised funds for the freedom fighters in Spain, and, in partnership with his son David, expanded his shoestring operation to half a dozen Harry W. Schwartz Milwaukee-area neighborhood bookstores. I was shocked to discover that the stores had been forced out of business by online book buying and electronic books since my last visit to Milwaukee, three years before.

Fortunately, a noted bibliophile and long-time buyer for the Harry W. Schwartz stores, Daniel Goldin, now owns and operates the Boswell Book Company in a former Schwartz location near Lake Michigan. On the night I visited Milwaukee, Daniel had invited the senior advanced-placement English class from a nearby high school to attend my event. Afterward, threading my way through the outskirts of town, hunting for a cheap motel, I found myself feeling nostalgic about my long-ago stint as a teacher. I was saddened, too, by the disappearance of the Harry W. Schwartz stores, though I knew that Harry and David would have been heartened to know that Daniel Goldin is continuing to provide very good books to the city made famous by several very good brews.

55
THE LEGACY, PART 1

Reg Bennett lived to be ninety. I visited him a few weeks before his death and was shocked to see how frail he'd become during the past several months. We drove up the mountain road above Chichester and, although he was too tired to get out, stopped at the pull-off beside the brook where he and my father and I had come in Dad's DeSoto to hear the Yankees–Red Sox games. And this was where, decades later, at the beginning of my book tour, the current property owner would offer me a job as a caretaker. Looking down the valley at his village, Reg asked if I thought that the manuscript of his Chichester stories was publishable. I said that it was and that I would see to it that *The Mountains Look Down* found a good home. Reg nodded. Then he said he had something important to tell me. After perhaps thirty seconds, during which neither of us spoke, he seemed to change his mind. All he finally said was, "You'll understand." A moment later he repeated himself. "You'll understand."

The envelope arrived by registered mail a few days after Reg's death. Inside was a copy of Reg's will, naming me as his principal heir, the recipient of his home and property. Like Pip's legacy in *Great Expectations,* it was an unexpected and valuable inheritance, particularly for a scrambling writer with two kids approaching college. I also inherited most of the contents of the house, including Reg's extensive library, with several first editions of Hemingway, Fitzgerald, and Thomas Wolfe, as well as his antique fly rods and his Chichester stories, for which I had promised to find a publisher. Yet as the leaves blew down that fall, and the Green Mountains turned gray for the long winter ahead, I felt sobered by the responsibility I had inherited. Reg had devoted his life to education. One way or another, I would use the inheritance for our children's education. And one way or another, I would find a way to publish Reg's stories.

One evening later that week our phone rang. The caller identified herself as the executor of Reg's will. "Of course," she said, "there is no property. Reg gave it all away."

I was stunned to learn that a few weeks before he died, Reg had turned over his house, his land, and most of his stock certificates to a young woman friend. I was told that he had given Margaret, as I'll call her, every last possession except for some furniture, the fly rods, his first editions, and the manuscript of *The Mountains Look Down,* which would still belong to me in accordance with the provisions of his otherwise invalidated will. But when, still in a state close to shock from my conversation with the executor, I called Margaret to inquire about the fly rods, books, and Chichester manuscript, she informed me that Reg had given them all away, as well. I was welcome to come and look through the house — now her house — she said. But I would find nothing.

I probably could not do anything to reclaim the house and property, even if I were disposed to try. But I had to find out what had become of Reg's memoir of our hometown.

Clearly, it was not going to be easy.

56
A PRAIRIE HOME BLOCKHEAD

There's a lot of human nature in all of us.
— GARRISON KEILLOR, *PONTOON*

I did not need a GPS to notify me that I was heading west again. Nor did I need a West Texas Jesus, an Oliver Sacks, or my deceased uncle to tell me that by doing so I was pressing my luck and the Loser Cruiser's. Probably I was pressing my luck by including Minnesota on my itinerary to begin with, given the highly problematic and personal nature of my mission. Nevertheless, I was determined to seek out Mr. Garrison Keillor, fellow author and host of the delightful *Prairie Home Companion* radio show, and, Red Sox cap in hand, apologize to him.

Dawdling along through the big woods of Aldo Leopold's and Laura Ingalls Wilder's Wisconsin, I half-hoped I'd be late arriving in St. Paul and therefore not have time for the apology before my event that evening. But like all of us sorry Lords of the Moss, yea, back to the peat dwellers themselves, no doubt, I am — for better or for worse — compulsively punctual. I hit St. Paul right on schedule in the late afternoon, with enough time to scout up Mr. Keillor and try to set things right between us.

To this day, I cannot think about this matter without the utmost mortification. Sackcloth and ashes don't begin to convey it. "Blockhead" is the word that springs to mind, and I don't mean the gracious Garrison K. Some years ago, a prominent Vermont bookseller invited Keillor to visit her store. She received this reply:

The last time I went to Vermont, there was a big outcry in the papers on account of a rumor that the show intended to move to Vermont. Vermonters were up in arms. I remember a comment from a distinguished Vermont writer named Howard Frank Mosher, who said, "This would be the last nail in the coffin for Vermont." I thought to myself, if it troubles Howard Frank Mosher so much to contemplate the possibility (nonexistent) that I might move to Vermont, then I don't need to visit Vermont again and cause Howard Frank Mosher all this trouble. If Vermont is troubled by outsiders, that's fine by me. I don't need to trouble anybody. In Minnesota, Howard Frank Mosher would be heartily welcomed, even if he wished to live here.

Oh, dear. The gentle irony. The devastating good humor. The sheer writerly *genius* of this kindly and unanswerable putdown to that churl from Vermont, Howard Frank Mosher. And then, wouldn't you know, it got up on the billion-tongued Net, where any damn body could, and did, Google it. Trouble was, rack my memory and conscience though I did, I couldn't remember saying such a thing. I enjoyed Keillor's Lake Wobegon novels and his show. I admired his tireless efforts on behalf of artists and the arts, not to mention his fine St. Paul bookstore, Common Good Books. Nor could I recall using the nail-in-the-coffin phrase. Gloomy, morbid, and dispiriting, it runs against my grain. Straightaway I wrote to Mr. Keillor, care of *Prairie Home Companion,* to apologize for the misunderstanding and exonerate myself. I received no reply.

Accordingly, and exactly as a person with a very guilty conscience would do, I wrote again. I hate self-exculpatory letters. So this time I admitted that, in a hideous, inexcusable lapse of manners and sanity, I *just might* have said that awful thing. The second letter — abject, reeking of the shameful "I'm sorry if you were offended" genre, as if anyone wouldn't be — was even worse than the first. Again, no response. "This Vermont character, Mosher, is a bad human being and a kook," I could hear Keillor's nice Lutheran secretary saying as she tossed the letter into the file marked "Bad Human Beings and Kooks." I had only one recourse left. I must *look up* Brother Garrison in the Land of 10,000 Lakes and personally apologize to him for what I was now 99.9 percent sure I'd said. Said out of pure, mean-spirited, smart-aleck, vicious, green-eyed jealousy. *If thy tongue offend thee, Harold, pluck it out.* Yes, yes, I'd do that, too, right on his show if he wanted me to. But perhaps the apology might suffice, and it would be nearly as painful.

GENERAL FICTION AND NON-FICTION, GOOD POETRY, CLASSICS ALL SIZES, QUALITY TRASH, announced the sign in the window of Common Good Books. Of course, Garrison had composed it. I laughed at "Quality Trash" despite myself, but the store, located in a small shopping area, is at the end of a long corridor that resembled nothing so much as Stephen King's Green Mile. Astonishingly, my own books were well represented there. Gathering them up to take to the counter to sign before asking directions to the *Prairie Home Companion* studio, I turned and nearly bumped into someone I recognized. I just couldn't think of his name. A middle-aged, midwestern-looking chap, very probably a walleye-eating minister, with a youthful cowlick and a benign countenance. My God. It was Garrison.

I took a deep breath and, with the do-or-die rapid-fire chagrin and unspeakable remorse of a wicked sinner at the pearly gates, I blurted out, "Mr.-Keillor-I'm-Howard-Frank-Mosher-and-I-owe-you-a-huge-apology-I'm-sure-I-did-say-that-bad-thing-about-you-coming-to-Vermont-and-out-of-context-it-must-have-sounded-even-worse."

On I blabbed, while kind, friendly, erudite Garrison, the host of *Prairie Home Companion,* the author of many funny novels, looked — puzzled. "I'm afraid I don't —" he started to say.

"No, no, no," I sputtered, waving, as if to avert an imminent train wreck. I was off and running again. Then I stopped.

Grinned. And said, "Hey, Garrison. I'm sorry I shot my stupid mouth off."

We shook hands. Mr. Keillor still seemed a bit baffled. "Excuse me," he said. "Who did you say you were?"

"Howard Mosher. Howard Frank Mosher? From Vermont?"

He shook his head. "I'm sorry, Mr. Mosher. I think you've mistaken me for someone else. My name's Fred Gustenson. I'm over from Thief River Falls for a convention. I came in here looking for a copy of *Eat, Pray, Love* for my wife."

57
IOWA CITY

Prairie Lights. What a gorgeous name for a novel or a poem or, in the case of downtown Iowa City's long-time literary gathering place, a bookstore. Prairie Lights Books is one of my favorite independents anywhere, but what did I encounter in Iowa City this Saturday afternoon but an angry outpouring from the university stadium, a vast army of the Hawkeye faithful, absolutely furious because their football team had just lost a conference game. The blasting horns, the squealing brakes, the snarls of starting-and-stopping SUVs — why did everyone in this pancake-flat prairie town need a four-wheel-drive SUV? — the scrumming melee and red-hot, palpable despair unique to disappointed college football enthusiasts and European soccer fans. And there in the catbird seat beside me, just when I least wanted to see him, was the West Texas Jesus, struggling to wrench the cap off a bottle of pale ale from an upscale local microbrewery with the seatbelt clip.

"You got a church key on you, bub?" he said.

I didn't, but he finally got the seatbelt clip to work, whereupon he chugged down half of that ale in three long gulps.

While we waited for the bottleneck outside the football stadium to clear, the West Texas Jesus picked up my copy of Marilynne Robinson's *Home,* on the front seat between us. "What's this about?" he asked.

As I told him about Robinson's Boughton and Ames families and the doomed attempts of Jack Boughton and his sister Glory to return to the rural Iowa village of Gilead to make new lives for themselves, he finished his ale and pried open another. Now he was riffling through Richard Dawkins's latest, *The God Delusion,* which I'd bought in Minneapolis at Garrison Keillor's Common Good Books.

I shut off the Cruiser so it wouldn't overheat in the traffic jam and, to make conversation, asked the West Texas Jesus which side of the debate over intelligent design he came down on. He thought a minute, then tapped the cover of the Dawkins book. "I'm a man of my times, I reckon. Always was — 'render unto Caesar,' et cetera. I don't have any big quarrel with this fella. Nothing in his book changes what I said about doing unto others, does it?"

I acknowledged that the theory of random natural selection, as I understood it, in no way contradicted the Golden Rule. But, connoisseur of paradoxes that he was, my old road bud wasn't finished. Holding his now nearly empty second pale ale up to the late-afternoon sunlight, as we finally started to creep forward, he said, "Then again, you ask me, *this* bad boy is the best evidence I know of a *very* intelligent de— SON OF MAN, HIT YOUR BRAKES!" I did. So did everyone else. All horns went silent. A cathedral quietude fell over the clogged main drag in front of the stadium. Not one $30,000 suburban vehicle moved an inch.

I craned my head out the Cruiser window. About a hundred yards ahead, a mama Canada goose was leading one, two, three, four, five, six, seven, eight, nine — count them, *nine* — fluffy yellow goslings from a second brood across the busiest street in Iowa that afternoon. Oh, America. Thoreau was surely right. The sun *is* a morning star. There *is* more day to dawn — randomly or otherwise.

58
UP IN MICHIGAN

Away up north in Petoskey, Michigan, where, as a boy, Ernest Hemingway summered with his family, I spent several happy hours the following afternoon walking the shore of the freshwater sea that is Lake Michigan. That evening, during the Q and A after my reading at Petoskey's excellent independent bookstore, McLean and Eakin, I related how I'd imitated first Hemingway and then Faulkner and then *both* of them.

In the spring of 1965, in the midst of struggling to find my own writing voice, getting my seniors ready for graduation, finishing my master's thesis, and dithering about the Pennsylvania fellowship and the rest of my life, I sat down one evening at the kitchen table to have another go at the novel I was trying to write. It was raining, the first soft spring rain of the year, the sort that stirs up the trout and makes them bite. For once, though, I wasn't thinking of fishing.

Some time passed, and suddenly I realized I had written the opening pages of my book. Not from Hemingway's point of view. Not from Faulkner's. From *mine.* "My father was a man of indefatigable optimism," I'd begun. And, though another fifteen years would elapse before I finished and published *Disappearances,* my first novel, I knew that with that sentence, I'd found my voice.

I jumped up and sprinted the three steps into our kitchen and read my pages aloud to Phillis. When I finished, she smiled and said, "Only in the Kingdom, sweetie."

59
THE LEGACY, PART 2

Not long after my aunt Elsie died, Reg visited his dentist for a checkup. A young female technician who had just started work there remarked that she had never met a person his age — he was in his early eighties — with such excellent teeth. Reg was smitten. From that day on, Margaret was all he could talk about. She was beautiful. She was an amateur golf star. It went without saying, though Reg did say it, and many times, that she was an expert dental technician. She was well traveled. And she was keenly interested in Reg's stories of Chichester and in Reg himself.

In due time Phillis and I met Margaret. She and Reg visited us in Vermont, and everything he had said about her appeared to be true. It was also true, as my father remarked, that around her, Reg acted like an infatuated teenager.

Margaret said little about herself, and only

very diffidently. There was, I thought, a certain watchfulness about her. I did not think then, nor do I now, that she was a gold digger. She was simply an attractive young woman who had formed a close friendship with a much older man. Reg had been miserably lonely since Elsie's death. He was not lonely now.

Over the next year, my uncle's infatuation with Margaret did not lessen. She told him that as a little girl on a camping trip to the ocean, she had seen her father drown. Reg acknowledged to me that Margaret probably perceived him as a replacement. At the same time, he hoped she might have romantic feelings for him. The following spring he returned to the Catskills after spending several months in Florida to discover that Margaret had married a man her own age. There were already serious problems with the relationship. Recently, she had discovered that her new spouse was an alcoholic. When Margaret wanted out of the marriage, Reg found her a lawyer and paid for her divorce. Several years later I made that last visit to the Catskills before his death, when he told me I would "understand." Then came his final illness, the arrival of the will, and, soon afterward, the brusque telephone call from the executor informing me that

Reg had deeded his house and property to Margaret just a few weeks before he died.

What distressed me most was the disappearance of the Chichester manuscript, *The Mountains Look Down*. In fact Reg wrote beautifully. I feared that those stories chronicling the history of our hometown might be lost forever — a loss that I found almost unbearable to contemplate. By contrast, my quest for the long-lost Canadian con-man novel I'd given away seemed trivial. All trace of Reg's stories seemed to have vanished as completely as the mountain characters he'd written about so lovingly, the long-defunct woodworking factory, and much of the village of Chichester itself. How could I fulfill my promise to Reg to publish *The Mountains Look Down* if I couldn't even locate the manuscript?

60
THE INDUSTRIAL BELT

Fess up, Harold. Prostate radiation treatment knocks the stuffing clean out of a guy. The first bombardment of rays tears the electrons off the molecules of the outer cells of the prostate and then, by the West Texas Jesus, that humming, behemoth X-ray machine rotates around and around you, zapping the now unprotected cancer cells and zapping, quite literally, the you-know-what out of your bowels. Oh, yes. Desperate situations do indeed require desperate remedies, and I will admit that, after forty-four rounds with Mr. Varian EX, followed by my zigzagging 20,000-mile odyssey through Bookland America, I was beat. I was counting the remaining days and wondering if I (and the LC) had the gas to get home.

Yet I still find it thrilling to drive through the muscular sprawl of industrial cities on the eastern fringe of America's Midwest.

How Walt Whitman would have loved the steel mills and railyards and automobile plants and petroleum refineries of Detroit and Gary and Erie and Cleveland and Cincinnati and Buffalo! The colossal football and baseball stadiums. The busy river barges and ingenious technological know-how that even in an economic recession keeps America going from one day to the next. Whitman would have known exactly what to say about all this. Any one of these Rust Belt cities would be likely territory for a young contemporary Whitman or Twain to stake out a claim and dig in. So, sure, go West, you aspiring poets and playwrights and novelists of early twenty-first-century America. Just remember, you don't need to go farther west than Buffalo if you don't want to. The great Buffalo novel? You bet.

As for me, when I walked into my friend Jonathon Welch's great Talking Leaves Books, in Buffalo, on the next-to-last day of my tour, and saw the colorful jackets of books that were my dear old acquaintances and books that might soon become new ones, I knew that wherever I have gone and might yet go, each time I step inside an independent bookstore I return again to the world of books, which has been my truest home for the more than sixty years.

■ ■ ■ ■

Back in Orleans in the uncertain spring of 1965, Phillis and I decided, with a few of our young teaching colleagues, to hold a huge end-of-the-school-year gala celebrating the history and literature of the Northeast Kingdom. One evening was dedicated to the kids reading their essays and stories on various topics: the Reverend Alexander Twilight, the African American graduate of Middlebury College who built the magnificent stone academy on the hill; Robert Rogers and his Rangers; Robert Frost's connection with the Kingdom; and the early Abenaki and French Canadian history of northern Vermont. The next night Jim Hayford read from his poetry and talked about his life and times in the Kingdom and beyond. Old-timers visited our classes and told stories about Prohibition and the Great Depression. The grand finale of this well-intended, if slightly deranged, frenzy of local culture, at a time when the kids should have been preparing for their finals, was an absolutely lunatic brainchild of my own devising.

Somehow, along with teaching, coaching, and story writing, not to mention finishing up my graduate thesis and embarking, with all the intrepidness of the absolutely clueless, on not one but *two* early attempts at book-length fiction — somehow I had found time to cajole our seniors into presenting, at the Orleans town hall on the final night of the Northeast Kingdom Weekend, a performance of *Our Town.* But not just any performance of *Our Town.* Nothing would do but, in keeping with the festival's local theme, I must doctor Thornton Wilder's masterpiece by adapting it to the Kingdom, with the assistance of my star pupil, Bill, and some of his classmates. Changing Grover's Corners to Orleans, not scrupling to substitute the names of real townspeople for characters in the play, and replacing the New Hampshire geography of *Our Town* with that of northern Vermont, we rehearsed night and day, planning to take the town by storm and finish up the Festival with a production that the good people of Orleans would never forget.

And to this day, they have not.

61
OUR TOWN

The town hall was the ideal venue for our project. With its heaving old wooden aisles, canted like the deck of a storm-tossed sailing ship, and its faded purple stage curtain redolent of mildew and the stardust of dozens of school and town plays and the brave collective hopes of scores of graduation valedictories — and let us not omit the bloody stains of not a few town-meeting brawls — the place was emblematic of our town. For a backdrop, the stage boasted several painted flats left over from a long-ago production of *Arsenic and Old Lace.* Teddy in his pith helmet, headed down cellar. The two patrician poisoner aunts, offering tea to an unsuspecting gentleman boarder. The mad doctor with his gleaming instruments of terror. In the disused orchestra well sat a piano once used to accompany silent movies, whose sole function for years had been to bang out, in hideous, off-key strains, the graduation march.

It's amazing how well Wilder's timeless play still reflects the human details of life in any American small town, and the hall was packed for the premiere. True, there was some ill-suppressed laughter when the curtain went up on the bare, stark stage, with the narrator — good old Bill — and the miming actors. But the audience was quickly drawn in by the stately rhythms of daily life in Grover's Corners, aka Orleans, and the substitutions of Kingdom names and anecdotes.

Soon it became apparent that *other* alterations had been made to the play, alterations I had not known about until now. These included references to old and current local love affairs, bitter feuds that had gone on for years, and the unsavory private habits, real or imagined, of a number of prominent Orleans citizens, including the local reverend, the mayor, the mill manager, some of us teachers, and old Prof. The audience began to murmur. A chill ran up my back as Big Prof, in the role of his father, came on stage staggering home from a school board meeting, muttering, "These Christly teachers aren't earning their pay. I'll get to the bottom of this or today isn't a three-quart day!"

Had the young rapscallions actually gotten their hands on some booze? The actors, now passing around a flask, were speaking directly to the audience about the townspeople's most private transgressions. Interactive theater had come to Orleans years ahead of the rest of the country. The mayor, a notorious alcoholic, lay passed out on the proscenium. The reverend's wife was picking the postmaster's pocket; the lecherous old business teacher had his hand on little Emily Webb's knee. What the hell was happening?

Up onto the stage rampaged the real Prof, red-faced, demanding that the production be halted, cuffing Big and Little, rushing from actor to actor like a mad bull. I ran onto the stage and shouted, "The play's the thing! It must go on."

Our undaunted leader had been drinking all afternoon, and his efforts to stop the presentation were ineffectual. Big and Little were laughing at their father. "Hand over that Christly flask," he roared, lunging for Big. The boys tossed the flask over Prof's head, behind their backs, under their legs, playing keep-away with it.

"Mosher, you crazy son of a bitch, stop this so-called play," Prof bellowed.

"The play must and will continue," I intoned. "Get back to your right lines, kids."

"No!" bayed Prof. Lowering his big round cannonball of a head, he came charging across the stage, determined to butt me into next Wednesday. Prof had several inches and a good hundred pounds on me. But I was young and wiry and brimming over with a whole school year of grievances against him and the board of education and authority in general. My employer's words of a year ago, at our teaching interview, flashed through my mind. "If you have to knock 'em down, make sure they stay down." As he charged me, trumpeting like a rogue elephant, I slipped aside and administered a swift, ungentle rap to his right ear, and he crashed head-first into the six-by-four-foot plywood flat of Teddy from *Arsenic and Old Lace.* Prof's head, sticking through the splintered hole in the flat, bore a striking resemblance to Teddy's. All my superintendent needed was a pith helmet.

"Waaah!" Prof roared. With the sheet of plywood still attached to his neck, he began to plunge around the crowded stage in a panic, scattering the young thespians.

"Dad! Hold still. What are you doing?" Big Prof shouted.

"Where's Mosher?" Prof shouted. "I'm going to kill Mosher."

School board members were hastening

down the aisles, making for the stage. That was fine by me. I'd give them a dose of the same, the cheapskates. Prof was swinging the plywood flat from side to side. Finally, he pushed the thing off his head.

I don't know what the audience thought. Later some claimed that they supposed Prof's antics and mine were part of the performance. Then a transformation seemed to come over the old administrator. Grinning hideously, he approached me, right hand extended. "I'm sorry, Mosher," he said. "I owe you an apology."

As he started to extend his hand, he said, "Oops. I dropped my hat."

He hadn't been wearing a hat, and that should have tipped me off. As he bent over to retrieve his nonexistent chapeau, I too bent over, and Prof delivered a tremendous uppercut to the side of my jaw. Miraculously, he didn't break it, but the blow lifted me off my feet and sent me sailing backward into the flat of the dear old-maid sisters. As I slid down it, I saw Prof collapsed facedown nearby. I was sure he was dead. Somehow, I had managed to murder the superintendent of schools. But no, he'd merely passed out. Students and school board members rushed hither and yon on the stage, which, Jim Hayford later remarked, resembled nothing so much as the body-strewn stage of the Globe Theater in the last scene of *Hamlet*.

Bill, the Middlebury-bound scholar and narrator of *Our Town,* put his arm under my shoulders and helped me to my feet. Some of the students laughed. Others applauded. Slowly, I raised a directorial finger.

"Ring down the curtain," I croaked out, and as someone blessedly did, I had the distinct impression that the curtain was about to come down on my short-lived career as a teacher as well.

"Not necessarily," Prof said to me a couple of nights later. His wife had kicked him out of the house temporarily, and he was holed up at the local hotel. "Up here in the Kingdom, folks will just respect both of us more after our little dust-up at the hall."

We sipped our beers, bought earlier that evening in the next town over. Prof grinned at me. "No hard feelings?"

"None," I said. After all, what was a little slugfest, in front of half the town, between fishing partners and friends?

"Remember when we went to get old Hayford's piano?" Prof said, chuckling.

"I do."

"That was a good time, wasn't it?"

"It was."

For the fourth or fifth time that evening, Prof put out his hand, and for the fourth or fifth time, somewhat warily, I shook it.

"Don't fall for that 'I dropped my hat' business again, okay?" Prof advised. "That's the oldest bar-fighting trick in the book."

"I won't," I said.

"So which do you think it'll be?" he asked, genuinely interested. "The University of Pennsylvania? Or another year here in the Kingdom?"

"I've been thinking about that," I said. "I can't really see myself as an Ivy League graduate student. Or as a professor at some college. Can you?"

Prof cracked open two more cold ones, shook my hand again, and looked me square in the eye. "Nope," he said. "I most surely cannot." And then, echoing Verna's words on the evening of the day Phillis and I got married, "Welcome home, my friend."

62
PAY DIRT

Like my uncle Reg, Francis Phelan, the on-the-skids hero of William Kennedy's novel *Ironweed,* was once a promising young baseball player. In *Ironweed* Kennedy evokes Depression-era Albany the way Reg evoked the Catskills in his own long-missing stories. Yet as I walked along Francis's Broadway, headed from downtown out toward the SUNY Albany campus, there were few signs of Kennedy's shabby old watering places where hard-nosed minor-league third basemen were lionized, aldermen bribed, union organizers shot and clubbed, and local stories spun into myth at a time when myth still mattered. Half-looking for Frankie Leikheim's plumbing shop, where Francis, marvelously, finds a piece of twine to tie up his flapping shoe, knowing that the only place I'd ever find it was between the covers of Kennedy's great novel, I wandered out to the university campus and sat down on a bench near the library.

Three hours before my final event, at the Book House of Stuyvesant Plaza, I was tired. Tired of the driving, the talks, the interviews. Tired from the aftereffects of my MacArthur Grant treatments, tired of the swirling memories of my life as a reader and writer. Disappointments from the Great American Book Tour? Not a one. I'd never supposed that canvassing the bookstores of America like a latter-day Willy Loman was going to make me a best-selling author. Only that the tour would help me reach whatever potential audience was out there for my stories, as indeed it had. When I'd left home, the late-spring woods of northern New England were still more gold than green. Now the trees on the SUNY Albany campus were starting to yellow again. My journey had encompassed parts of three seasons.

You'd think that a writer would be temperamentally introspective, if not outright introverted. Actually, I've always found other people's stories to be more interesting than my own. For decades my working life has consisted of sitting down at the kitchen table every morning and filling up yellow legal tablets. My fellowship temporarily emancipated me from that regimen. It allowed me the time to take a trip I had long wished to make and also to take inventory of my own life at a critical juncture.

True, I hadn't found the elusive Canadian novel I'd been looking for for thirty-some years. But what the hey. This close to a university library, why not try once more?

I went in, poked around in the fiction section, and scanned some *New Yorker* reviews from the fall of 1977, when I was pretty sure the con-man book had been published. Nothing. Then I checked the baseball scores and standings in William Kennedy's former newspaper, the *Times Union.* I was thinking about baseball, Uncle Reg, and, fleetingly, my canceled legacy, when the dimmest of dim recollections flared up in the recesses of my mind. It was as if some part of me *knew* something of tremendous importance that I hadn't yet consciously processed. I walked over to the information desk. How far back, I inquired, did the library's files of SUNY Albany master's theses go? The young man at the desk wasn't sure, but after I explained what I was looking for, he punched the name I gave him into his computer, made a quick note to himself, and told me he'd be back.

At length the librarian returned with a cardboard box. "Is this by any chance what you're looking for?"

The flaps, as I recall, were fastened with twine, like the twine Francis Phelan found on Broadway to tie up his poor broken shoe. Inside, wrapped neatly in plain brown paper, was a hefty manuscript. The title page read "The Mountains Look Down: A Study of a Catskill Village. A Thesis Presented to the Faculty of the N.Y. State College for Teachers in Partial Fulfillment of the Requirements for the Degree of Master of Education. By Reginald R. Bennett." What followed was, as nearly as I could determine, Reg's long-missing history of Chichester. It began with the stately, assured cadences I remembered from my early boyhood when Reg first read me his stories: "In the winter of 1863, a man came west from the Hudson River, traveling by easy stages, and slowly, with horse and sleigh, to the foothills of the Catskills." I could scarcely believe it. Searching for one book, I had found another, infinitely more precious and personal. I had found the book whose stories, so long ago, had inspired me to write my own. The stories that I had supposed to be lost forever.

The manuscript was about five hundred pages long. The librarian ran off a copy for me, for which I paid thirty dollars — the last cash in my wallet. Then I walked out of the library into the cool fall evening with my legacy.

63
RESOLUTION

How do you know when you've finished a story? In real life, after all, stories tend not to have well-defined endings. There is always one more thing to tell. And that is true in the case of Reg's legacy. Up on that mountainside looking down on the village of Chichester before he died, just prior to Reg telling me he had something important to say and then apparently changing his mind, he asked me a question.

"Howard, do you think Margaret loves me?"

I am far from proud of some of the things I did and said and thought in regard to the matter of my disinheritance. But I am glad to report that, in reply to this question, I said, without hesitation, and meaning it as much as I've ever meant anything, "Yes. I know she does."

Reg nodded. I believe that may have been the moment when he made up his mind what to do with his property. Certain mysteries remain, as they are apt to with true stories. Where *did* Reg's fly rods and first-edition books and manuscript go? Why did Margaret get married and divorced in less than a year? What was the true nature of Reg's undeniable love for her and hers for him? Was she a surrogate daughter? Were they lovers? I'll never know. The point is that Reg had trusted me to understand his decision.

At last I did.

64
HOMECOMING

I didn't sleep much that night at my Motel 6 in Albany. I was too excited about discovering Reg's book and about going home. Around three a.m. I got up for good and headed north. Up through the dark foothills of the Adirondacks and on into the Green Mountains of Vermont. The two-lane mountain road coming into Irasburg from the west cuts across a saddle, where I pulled over to watch the sun rise on the Kingdom. From here, in the chilly September dawn, I could hear the factory whistle in Orleans, five miles to the east. *Welcome home, Moshers. Keep the kids out of the mill.*

I could see the woods northeast of town where, long ago, Verna made moonshine to feed her family and save her farm.

Closer by was the village where Phillis and I have now lived for more than thirty years, with its brick store and post office and scattering of white houses around the common.

Just south of the green sits our old farm-house. And, between the foot of the moun-tain and the town, the cemetery where, a few weeks before I left for the Great Ameri-can Book Tour, Phillis and I bought our plot and commissioned a bench with our names and birth dates and a heart carved between them.

Snap.

I looked to my right and there he was in the catbird seat, cracking open his first tall boy of the morning.

"I was hoping you'd show up again," I said. "Back in Montana when you made off with my fly rod? What was it you called out to me when I asked you about the unfin-ished business with my uncle?"

The West Texas Jesus raised his Corona to me and then, if I'm not mistaken, to the panoramic vista of the Northeast Kingdom spread out before us in the sunrise. "What I said," he told me, "was go back to the Kingdom and write about it."

And with that he slipped away, leaving me to drive the last mile home to Phillis.

65
THE APOCRYPHAL BOOK
OF HAROLD

A few weeks after he got back to Vermont, Harold Who located a fine regional publisher specializing in Catskill Mountain history and literature, and in due time his uncle's book, *The Mountains Look Down,* was well published and enthusiastically received.

At about the same time that Reg's book came out, I discovered, through ABE.com, that damnable Canadian novel, a picaresque romp called *Farthing's Fortune.* I am delighted to report that I liked it just as much as I had three decades before.

Monty the snake got thirsty and came out of the ductwork. To celebrate, I ordered for Phillis a life-size stuffed emperor penguin from Anderson's Bookstore in Naperville, Illinois. Also, I presented her with an eight-by-eleven framed photograph of me reading to several of his feathery brood one rainy night on the outskirts of Chicago. It is my favorite photograph from the Great American Book Tour.

I still have not heard from Garrison Keillor. But after apologizing to Fred Gustenson, I feel that I have done about as much as I can.

The jury is *still* out on the long-term results of my MacArthur Fellowship. It always is, with any kind of cancer. So far so good, however, and as my friend from West Texas might and, come to think of it, did once say, sufficient unto the day is the evil thereof. To which I will take the liberty of adding, the joy of the day as well.

$25. RUNS GOOD. DEMO DERBY?

This, of course, was Phillis's idea. The day after I got home from the book tour, we stuck the sign on the catbird-seat window of the Loser Cruiser, now parked on the front lawn. Within five minutes, two pickups had pulled into our driveway and four teenage boys were kicking its tires and squabbling about who'd gotten there first. The Cruiser took second in the preliminary heat of that year's demolition derby at the Orleans County Fair, a fitting Kingdom County conclusion to a remarkable twenty-year run.

ABOUT THE AUTHOR

Howard Frank Mosher is the author of ten novels and two memoirs.

The employees of Thorndike Press hope you have enjoyed this Large Print book. All our Thorndike, Wheeler, and Kennebec Large Print titles are designed for easy reading, and all our books are made to last. Other Thorndike Press Large Print books are available at your library, through selected bookstores, or directly from us.

For information about titles, please call:
   (800) 223-1244

or visit our Web site at:
   http://gale.cengage.com/thorndike

To share your comments, please write:
   Publisher
   Thorndike Press
   10 Water St., Suite 310
   Waterville, ME 04901